The Dawn of Awakening

www.thedawnofawakening.com

Thank you

Richard Bach, Babaji, Buddha, Rhonda Byrne, Gregg Braden, Carlos Castaneda, Deepak Chopra, Ram Dass, Leonardo DaVinci, JJ Dewey, Albert Einstein, Masaru Emoto, Micheal Gelb, Nassim Harmain, Vito Hemphill, John Lennon, C.S. Lewis, Barbara Marciniak, Valdimir Medre/Anastasia, Leonard Orr, George Orwell, Ayn Rand, James Redfield, Eckhart Tolle, Neil Donald Walsh, and many more who have been an inspiration for this work.

1ˢᵀ BINDING- JUNE 2012

Author's Limited Edition
ISBN 978-0-9851049-1-7

Published by

G&H Press

518 Santa Fe Trail #400
Santa Fe, NM 87505

Artwork by Heather Ligresti

**Printed in the USA using Recycled Paper
and vegetable-based ink**

The Manual of Spiritual Living

Part 1: The Dawn of Awakening

Gio & Heather Ligresti

The Manual of Spiritual Living answers these questions and more:

What is Spirituality?

Do I go with the flow?

What are miracles?

Should I stop having judgement?

How can I increase my potential?

Are we all connected, and if so, to what?

What can I do to save the planet?

How do I create the outcomes that I desire?

I really enjoy comfort and abundance, does that mean that I am not a Spiritual person?

Can I still keep my after-life insurance with God if I take charge of my own Spirituality?

The Manual of Spiritual Living

Part 1: The Dawn of Awakening

Part 2: The Eve of Transformation

Part 3: Love is Union

and more to come

www.themanualofspiritualliving.com

A tale often told, mostly to demonstrate the subjective nature of truth, is the story of the six blind men and the elephant. Each of the blind men stand in front of the elephant and attempt to determine what an elephant looks like by feeling different parts of the elephant's body. The blind man who feels a leg says the elephant is like a pillar; the one who feels the tail says the elephant is like a rope; the one who feels the trunk says the elephant is like a tree branch; the one who feels the ear says the elephant is like a hand fan; the one who feels the belly says the elephant is like a wall; and the one who feels the tusk says the elephant is like a solid pipe.

The king explains to them:

"You are all right. The reason each one of you is telling it differently is because you have all touched a different part of the elephant. The elephant has all of the features you mentioned."

This is supposed to resolve the conflict, and the story is used to illustrate the principle that truth can be stated in different ways. We feel, however, that this tale is better used to demonstrate how humans are stuck, not in their misunderstanding of what the truth is, but in the way that they approach the truth. If each of these men would have kept their hands moving and continued their search until they were reasonably sure that they had observed the entire elephant, none of them would have given such a silly description. And this is often the way humans approach things, they draw conclusions too quickly before having a whole picture. Humans are lazy when it comes to searching for the truth and too often stop at the first glance, or in the case of the blind men and the elephant, at first touch. The second mistake that these men make, which is mirrored by humans, is that they do not communicate with one another to find out what the others are discovering. If two findings contradict one another then the search is not over. These men could have communicated with one another and shown the various parts to one another in order for them all to have a better idea of what an elephant actually looks like.

Had these men kept looking, and communicated with one another, all six of them would have had a very good idea of what an elephant actually looks like. Truth is unchanging, like the elephant, but how one approaches the truth will change ones perception of it. The greatest lesson of this tale is not that the truth is unable to be found, on the contrary, the lesson is that the truth is found from an impeccable search and an open communication with others who are searching for the like!

From *"The Manual of Spiritual Living, Part 2: The Eve of Transformation"*

＆

"Awakening is the act of consciously waking up the dormant consciousness within. As we awaken, we become aware that what we know is not limited to what we have learned or experienced throughout this lifetime."

~ Gio & Heather

ç

Contents

CONTENTS

ENDNOTE
page 190

ABOUT THE AUTHORS
page 192

6

Author's Preface

As a loving couple, we have been able to teach and learn from one another. Love is our Spiritual Guide, and it is through our union that we have experienced our most powerful and profound Spiritual experiences. Our Spiritual Journey is one that is fun, easy-going, loving and free. We believe that Spirituality is not about unnecessary sacrifice; instead, it is a path of pleasure and joy overruled by an impeccable commitment to the truth and doing what is right.

After experiencing many years filled with an abundance of love, joy, healing, miracles, truth, and understanding, we got a clear inspiration that the two of us were going to write a book about our Spiritual Path. These books are written with the precise purpose and the clear intention to make this world a better place and to help humans transform into a more evolved expression of themselves.

Written on the pages of these books are all of the tools and information to help humanity to reach their next level of evolution, where they can live in harmony with each other and with the planet as intentional Beings. Our power as humans lies within our ability to co-create this world. This book facilitates the awakening process to bring humans more in touch with the part of them that is an intentional co-creator. It helps to see through the veils of illusion and teaches the great art of manifestation.

Yoga has been a very inspirational source for many of the teachings in this book. The Yoga Path is a much more encompassing philosophy than the intentional movements

7

which most people know it for. This book is a Yoga Practice for the mind.

Our understanding of Spirituality means prioritizing the search for truth regarding the understanding of humans and who they are apart from their body and their productivity in the physical realm. We wrote these books with the intent of awakening others and to help them find the courage to live their physical experience as protagonists of their destiny rather than victims of the events.

We believe that if one is completely true to their Highest Self all of our paths will eventually lead us to the same place.

There are people that believe in the existence of higher powers and there are those who do not. The Spiritual Path is simply a path of impeccability. It is a path of personally taking responsibility to reach the highest expression that we can conceive of - the path is one of Conscious Intentional Evolution. This path is for all those who choose to be the protagonists of a continuos improvement of the human species and all that humanity comes in contact with.

The Spiritual Journey is one that is ongoing. Our commitment to truth is our highest priority, so we are open, expectant and even hopeful that new information will lead us to new outlooks and even more enlightened interpretations. Our goal is not to impersonate someone else to follow while guiding others on the "right" path; instead, our goal is to help the Spiritual growth of those humans, who like us, are highly committed to the growth of their evolution as Spiritual Beings while on a human journey.

Hopefully together with you we will reach higher and higher understandings as a family of luminous Beings, and shine our light over all who feel drawn to and driven by love and truth.

With Gratitude and Love,

Gio & Heather Ligresti
Santa Fe, NM
May 2012

Dedicated to you, the reader,

with gratitude.

1

SPIRITUALITY:
THE ULTIMATE UNION

When the curiosity for the Spiritual mystery is accompanied by a sense of responsibility to become part of the process of finding truths regarding Spirituality, choosing to embrace it is the conscious thing to do. This means choosing to commit ourselves to make our whole life into a Spiritual Adventure rather than merely experiencing scattered Spiritual moments within our life. Instead of finding Spirituality in between chores we can make Spirituality our constant state of mind in which all of our chores reflect our commitment to Spiritual Evolution.

This Spiritual Journey will take us into all aspects of human living and it will encourage us to scrutinize all that we think we know because of our chosen commitment to find truth also when this truth resides hidden inside unquestionable places deep within us. There are shells that form and protect beliefs when we deem these beliefs unquestionable. These shells create pockets of darkness shadowed, protected and undisturbed by the unwillingness to question everything, and therefore expose everything to the light of truth. The Spiritual path is a path of Intentional Conscious Evolution. Evolution is transformation, transformation is a process of change, and constructive intentional change demands that everything can be questioned. All that gets buried does not receive light, and what we uncover we bring into the light. This unraveling process has the potential to remove the layers[1] which entrap the light and shadow the truth, thereby unlocking human potential.

The most important way that we know to achieve Ultimate Union with the Divine consists of becoming impeccable with our behavior. We believe that the most powerful way to honor the Divine is by behaving with the same integrity, commitment, impeccability, compassion, rightfulness, determination, courage, and dedication to truth as we would imagine the Divine would display.

Many humans unquestionably accept that perfection is unattainable to them. The assumption is that perfection can only be found in God and seeking to mirror such perfection is considered an arrogant form of blasphemy. This causes humans to accept and maintain their state of imperfection as a form of respectful inferiority. This respectful inferiority becomes a self-condemnation to remain forever within the boundaries of inferiority and imperfection.

---

1   See: Ch. 6, Shedding the Layers, pg. 58

Honoring God by respecting this inferiority then becomes a justification for the lack of impeccability behind all behaviors and all endeavors.

Walking a Spiritual path, in our definition, means to choose the path of Intentional Conscious Evolution as the ultimate way to honor the Divine. We believe in living life, not as victims of an orchestrated Universe, but as the protagonists of our future. We believe that whether or not we can achieve the same heights as the Divine does not need to be a deterrent for trying, but rather a stimulant to push us towards higher states of Spiritual Evolution. It seems more objective and instinctively more inspirational for us to conceive of a potentially unlimited Spiritual Growth, rather than growth restricted by the need of superiority which many attribute to the Divine.

Superiority and inferiority are simply adjectives to express a measurement of something— not a way to maintain separation. In other words, an extremely evolved and evolving Being will maintain their ongoing evolutionary process, and rather then feel threatened or disrespected by other Beings focused on their path of evolution they will feel happiness and joy to know that other Beings are working their way towards them on the evolutionary ladder. In our understanding of the Spiritual Evolutionary Process, the more distance there is in evolution between Beings and the more lonely it can be. The more Intentional Spiritual Beings one can find on a similar path and at a similar level of Evolution and the more the Spiritual Adventure becomes desirable. Since all Beings are interconnected, including

Divine Beings, these Super-Evolved Beings will benefit as a consequence of others' Spiritual Evolution. Spiritual Evolution is also measured by ones capacity to discern the differences in evolution between Beings without indulging in unnecessary negative emotions.

Spirituality entails walking the path inspired by the highest vision of greatness and offering all the greatness within ourselves in return for this inspiration.

The goal is not to enter into a petty competition with what one can conceive of as the 'Ultimate Evolution'. One is honoring their commitment to evolution itself by offering all that they have to offer without holding back. We expect that a highly Evolved Being would not be wrapped up in their ego and consider our actions to be inappropriate or arrogant; instead, they would feel honored by this total commitment to Spiritual Evolution itself. The rational, likely reaction that we expect a Being of an exceptional evolutionary state to have when witnessing our impeccable, rightful, and good intentions would be one of pride and joy. Similarly would an evolved parent have such feelings when observing like behavior in their children.

There are many associations between the Divine and the Light. Instead of indulging in being a tiny reflection of the *light*, we focus on becoming a source of *light*. Rather than fearing the effects of the consequential increase in radiance, we enjoy and honor the contribution that we are now offering by becoming part of this en*light*ening process and offering our own luminosity.

Accomplishing, or even attempting, such a grand task as becoming our highest self, including doing it for the purpose of connecting with the Divine requires a constant commitment. This commitment is honored by finding the connection between Spirituality and all of life's endeavors. Practicing Spirituality as one added endeavor means that the commitment to Spirituality will be limited to only a small percentage of our Being and the implication is that there is no need and no use for an Intentional Spiritual Attitude to overlook all of our actions. Only by taking it upon ourselves to impersonate the Divine, by acting impeccably, will we become intentional co-creators.

The act of becoming impeccable in ones intentions, and consequently in all actions, endeavors, judgements, decisions, and choices is the responsibility adopted by a Being wanting to be the protagonist of making themselves a better Being and participate in becoming part of the solution to make the Universe a better place. Becoming better is accomplished by being intentional about doing the right thing at all times. Doing the right thing at all times requires having the commitment and the courage to determine what is right[2] using a combination of impeccable objective reasoning and true compassion. We consider the act of walking a Spiritual Path very similar to walking a path

---

2   See: Ch. 12, Right is Right, pg. 104

of impeccability— the highest form of commitment towards the Spirit is honored by the amount of impeccability that one is willing to adopt. This path is the most likely path to lead to whatever Spiritual Truth may exist and/or to the embodiment of the Spiritual Truth itself.

The first thing that we recommend when approaching an Intentional Committed Spiritual Path is to reach the awareness of who one is underneath the layers and layers of inherited beliefs which most humans have been taught to believe represent who they are. **The commitment to find out who we are is not for the sake of maintaining that image as another sacred unchangeable truth; it is only the starting point to become who we decide to be.** That is Intentional Evolving Beings whose efforts are dedicated to the highest good. This means becoming intentional towards our evolution.

We believe that a Spiritual path is not limited to those who believe in the existence of the "Spirit"; it is for all those who want to start the journey in which they will explore the possibilities of Spirit without being bounded by other peoples beliefs. The word Spirituality, however, implies the existence of another layer of existence beyond what is physical. What we believe is important is to focus at least as much attention in becoming Impeccable Intentional Beings for the sake of goodness as in looking for the existence of an outer form of Spirit. Entering a Spiritual Adventure is not the same as adopting a Religious belief. Spirituality is an adventure because one can approach it with an objective and curious mind, without having the burden of other people's beliefs and expectations.

We all are Spiritual Beings on a human journey.

Spirituality is the conscious and impeccable seek for the truth regarding our Spiritual Self and the conscious and impeccable attempt to find and share enlightenment by combining our intuitive and rational capacities. In other words, Spirituality is the impeccable search for truth guided by intuition and objectivity. The Spiritual path is a path that encompasses awakenings, and Living-Aware. Awakening[3] is a process of remembering without the restrictions that come from our domestications[4]. Living-Aware means being present and diligently observing every aspect of our life with an open mind and an open heart. Many people spend most of their time in planning the future, and while doing so they pay little or no attention to the present. Planning the future reflects an active mind and a heightened sense of responsibility, however being present and enjoying life is what Spiritual Seekers strive to accomplish. One can learn to balance the enjoyment of living in the present moment with dedicating a reasonable amount of time to planning a beautiful future.

The seek for truth in regards to the Divine is a seek that when approached with impeccability is motivated by love. This means that the highest motive

---

3   See: Chapter 24, Awakening, pg. 180
4   See: Chapter 22, Domestication, pg. 160

that an Intentional Spiritual Seeker has to honor is to connect with their highest vision of greatness as an act of love. Love is the ultimate motive for all unions, whether with other Beings, ourselves, or the Divine.

2

WE ARE WHO WE CHOOSE TO BE

The main objective of *The Manual of Spiritual Living* is to help humans in the process of awakening, transformation and union. The meaning of Spiritual Evolution can be explained as Intentional Transformation of the Spiritual Self. In this chapter we bring awareness to some of the important issues that slow Human Beings from their Spiritual Evolution. The main factor is the belief that it is important to defend who they think they are. When Human Beings focus their attention on defending who they think they are, they are defending themselves from change. This includes the act of becoming who they want to become.

We are Intentional Beings, which means we intentionally and continuously choose who we want to be.

This statement is a treasure and we highly recommend that every Human Being on a Spiritual Journey honor it. Let it be a constant reminder that will always preserve an outlook upon oneself as the person in charge of leading their own path; and, one who will never succumb to the passive approach of being stuck in a non-evolving paradigm.

Many people can spend their entire lives pondering about *who they are*, without thoughtful consideration about *who they want to be*. Even though *who you are* can be a worthy thing to give your attention to, in reality, the idea of *who you are* is mostly a construct of the ego and can take you away from your Enlightened Spiritual Path. The ideas that *we are this* or *we are that* are truly some of the biggest illusions that separate people. If we remember that we are Evolving Beings, then we can remember not to identify with who we think we are today. The journey of knowing oneself, and one's short and long comings is a journey of wiseness.

A Spiritual Seeker needs to remain focused on what they want to become, rather than stuck on what they are today. We are not the same person as we were 20 years ago, 10 years ago, 5 years ago, or even yesterday. If we were to remain unchanged, that would be a sign that we are not evolving, since evolution requires change. Evolving is part of this beautiful journey, so how much we change through the course (yes, course like in school terms) of our life is also a measurement of how much we have accomplished in terms of our evolution. We, on our journey, have been undergoing a rapid amount of change in our years. Looking back to who we used to be is beautiful, because we can still see our highest selves that were always there, and we also see our human selves that have learned and changed in the years. Most of all, we look forward to becoming our more evolved future selves.

Our commitment to intentional change combined with impeccability in motives bring about Conscious Evolution. Over and over in life we face choices and multiple factors intervene and influence these choices. These factors include our reactions to the feelings of fear[5], envy, jealousy, and anger. The choices that we make will have an effect on us, and on others. Our commitment as Intentional Spiritual Beings is to act according to the highest vision of who we want to be. This motivates us to act as Impeccable Beings who constantly seek out truth, strive to become better Beings and actively participate in making this world a better place.

The first step is to acknowledge all of the emotions involved in making the choices. This means acknowledging the feelings of fear as an unpleasant but necessary tool of awareness. Next we impeccably focus our attention on making the right choices. This means making our commitment to what is right the driving force behind all of our decisions. Our intention is to honor our highest self at all times, and assure that what steers us towards our choice is courage and love.

---

5   See: Chapter 5, Fear, pg. 48

Acknowledging how negative emotions affect us means to acknowledge our weaknesses. Weaknesses are there not to be left alone or upheld, but rather to be faced and dealt with. This internal search will bring us to become more aware of feelings that we are not proud of and that we often intentionally try to ignore, as they expose a part of us to ourselves which is not who we want to be. An example can be the feeling of dislike towards those people who have something that one would like to have but does not have. Rather than indulging in the feeling of dislike towards them, and soaking in the frustrated, negative energy or even rather than denying and repressing the negative emotions— one can arise into a feeling of loving acceptance. Remember, the main purpose is to choose who one wants to be. Wanting to be a loving Being helps to find a place within oneself where one can soak in the love energy, as opposed to indulging in a dislike and hatred state of mind. This will likely increase the chances that one's impact toward the people they feel envy towards will be positive and the connection with them will be beneficial and constructive for all.

We are taught that in order to be "somebody" we need to be acknowledged by others as such. This teaching requires us to become somebody that other people will be able to recognize within a category. In other words, in order to become somebody, we have to become somebody else's understanding of "special". On the other hand, there are other teachings which tell us that we are already special, and that there is nothing that we need to do in order to become somebody special in the eyes of others.

These two approaches, to become somebody or not become somebody, both lack impeccability of intentions. The first step in becoming somebody special, special being a positive outlook of ourselves, is by becoming committed to continuously better ourselves. Part of the process in doing that is having the courage to evaluate whether our definition of "better" is the result of pure intentions. Both spread teachings mentioned above offer a comfortable goal to reach, as the result of others appreciation, either for doing something or for not doing anything. Humans have the capacity to appreciate comfort and what we would like to offer is a perspective for which comfort is a desirable result in a much deeper and more profound way. That is the result of becoming a special somebody in our own eyes after having managed to transform the person behind those eyes into an Impeccable Being dedicated to the highest good.

Many people believe they are what they were taught to be. The process of shedding the layers[6] allows a person to expand into their higher self. Most humans do not actively participate in the process of actually deciding who they are. For the most part, humans have merely accepted to be what others wanted them to be and what they found themselves to be. They have not consciously chosen the color of their skin, their physical attributes, their Religion, their cultural customs, etc. Likely they have not even consciously chosen the political party they find themselves voting for. The vast majority of their opinions on what is right and what is wrong probably came from the opinions of

---

6   See: Chapter 6, Shedding The Layers, pg. 58

the majority of people around them. In other words, **most humans are busy defending who they are as a result of other people's influences, rather than defending their innate right to really become the protagonists of themselves.**

It is a common behavior for humans to point fingers towards other humans who are covering a position of power and decision making. This behavior suggests that the people towards which the fingers are pointed to are the essence of all problems. The problem, however, is usually shared by the lack of impeccability within both those that are pointing the fingers and those towards which the fingers are pointed. In the present-day scenario, economy has become one of the leading powers to control human society. The business leaders are typically chosen based on their capacity to generate a profit. Those pointing fingers criticize this criteria; and the implication is that consciousness is being neglected. The behavior of neglecting consciousness for personal comfort, whether in the form of profit or in other forms of egotistical self-prioritization, is a problem that Human Beings commonly share regardless of whether they are in a position of power or not. It is this behavior that we believe we aught to focus on to improve all Human Beings. Accumulating wealth in and of itself is not the problem. The problem is with all of the acts of prioritizing self comfort, including the act of accumulating wealth without consciousness of the consequences towards others and the Earth. The prioritization of the comfort zone is just as much an obstacle.

The leaders of the World Economy reflect the lack of true consciousness which has been commonly accepted by Human Beings as part of their "Human Nature". Since business leaders have been chosen for their capacity to make a profit, it becomes the driving force behind what they do along with the decisions that they make. Instead, if they were behaving more consciously, they would also focus on the impact that their decisions have on all others, thus giving it the same importance that they give to making a profit. Generating wealth in a healthy, conscious manner would remain an important and respectable part of their job, just not at the expense of others and the Earth.

◈

Humans have been mislead to focus their attentions on being good at what they do. The most important thing, however, is that what they do is good.

◈

The same people who are pointing the fingers often perceive themselves as victims of others; meanwhile they neglect their own personal impact. They assume that voting for someone else to make things right or diverting their responsibilities onto God is the way to free themselves from further obligation. Or, some believe that complaining about their misery is all that their part calls for. This is simply not true. Humans are not merely grains of sand in a vast desert. They are the protagonists of their lives and the co-creators of this world. **Our size and number are not the only factors that determine the scope and the**

power of our influence. Our actions and our choices are more important than the vote given to somebody else to hopefully make the right choices.

If we want the world to change, we have to be willing to change ourselves first.

We have to become the change[7]. These are not meant to be words spread in the wind. The constructive approach to these words will have an effect only when people will act according to their higher selves. Becoming impeccable means that we will not be accepting of ourselves as those who do "*some*" things right. If we accept ourselves to be the ones who are only responsible for doing "some" things right, then we are also accepting ourselves to be the ones who do "some" things wrong. There is no consistency in expecting others, that we have directly or indirectly allowed or supported to cover a place of power, to do everything right when we allow ourselves the luxury to be less than impeccable. The amount of wrongdoing can never be clear to those who dwell in a belief system for which wrongdoing is acceptable. It becomes another layer upon layer of adjustments which blanket and obscure the effects of our lack of integrity and the consequential pain and suffering that this ends up causing ourselves and others.

We have heard many people defending their right to be who they think they are while expressing that they themselves were not perfect. Since each and

---

7   Mahatma Gandhi is said to say a similar phrase, "Be the change you want to see in the world."

every individual is responsible for choosing who they want to be, then accepting this responsibility requires us to strive for the constant seek for perfection[8].

Being who we choose to be means being aware that humans tend to adapt their behavior in accordance to what works in the context of the society and the environment. It is also thanks to this capacity of adaptation that Human Beings have survived on the planet. The more a society grows in complexity and the more complex become the requirements for one to become functional in that society. For example, humans are born naked and the presumption is that clothes are a necessary item to keep us warm; instead clothes have grown into a much more complex part of the human life. Wearing clothes is not a choice anymore, but a requirement; it is illegal in most places around the world to be without clothing. Clothing is also a costume with which one communicates. It may identify what job one does, how wealthy one is, what political ideas one has, what religious views one has, what environmental issues one has, and much more.

The ongoing layers of complexity in behaviors and rules within the ongoing complexities of society are continuous tests to both the capacity of adaptation of the individual, and the identification of the individual within the expectations of the society. Humans are the most domesticable animal that we know of, and that is what makes them capable of creating societies in which an enormous number of people have access to food, shelter and much more. An example of how domesticable humans are is in the fact that they are probably the only animal on the planet that can sit on an airplane for 15+ hours without a leash or a cage restraining them. This is an admirable capacity, but at the same time, this capacity also allows for the placement of layers upon layers of domestications[9] which cover our intentional selves.

Society teaches people to continuously manipulate their interactions with others in order for that interaction to bring them some kind of personal gain. Domestication often makes humans find themselves in situations where they feel pressured to play the part that they have been taught to play in order to keep others in their comfort zone, rather than honor and express to others who they want to be. These unwritten codes of behaviors, which humans tend to follow, are derived from a number of factors (culture, religion and also many fear related issues). Following these codes will often result in achieving a popular status, as these codes have become a successful, yet dysfunctional, way to interact with the society.

Humans have been domesticated to be fearful of others. Many have been exposed to the phrase, "no one does something for nothing." That is simply not true. We actually enjoy doing many little things for the sake of helping others; in fact, we highly recommend for an individual on a Spiritual path to fill life with many, many spontaneous acts of kindness. Perhaps, in some ways, we do get something back as doing good things can make one feel good. The intention, however, is to

---

9   See: Chapter 22, Domestication, pg. 160

do good things for the sake of being good, not for something in return.

We have discovered domestications encoded deep within Human Beings that include the belief that humans are doomed to be victims of their humanity. This implies that their humanity is the barbaric representation of themselves. This unkind, constrictive, and diminishing perspective guides their actions to be driven by a desire to obtain something at someone else's expense. Our conclusion is that this social domestication has become responsible for an overly suspicious attitude towards other's expressions of kindness.

We have found ourselves expressing kindness in many different forms on many different occasions. Before offering a charitable action we first deeply evaluate our motives. On some occasions, even after establishing that our motives were impeccable, we still have found ourselves confronted with other people's suspicions. There have been times in which we have wondered whether in order to express our kindness more successfully, we should have submitted ourselves more to the unwritten rules that exist within the interactions of Human Beings.

These unwritten rules represent a way of communicating which is more easily understood but at the same time, these rules force one to play a part. We believe that being able to express kindness for the sake of goodness is an important objective. We are also aware of the creation of unwritten rules within the society which allow people to play a part while interacting with each other without distorting their comfort zones and harboring fearful feelings. Nevertheless, we also want to honor who we are outside of the box within which people want to place us for their comfort. On some occasions we found ourselves deciding whether or not to express an act of generosity when such an act could be interpreted as suspicious by strangers. Those who know us have an amazing amount of trust in us, since they are familiar with the impeccable way that we choose to live. Our acts of kindness, however, are often expressed to people that we are meeting for the very first time.

Our conclusions regarding this subject are that the priority for an Intentional Spiritual Seeker is to behave as the person they want to be above what other people want them to be. The results may vary depending on a number of factors, but in general, acting in accordance to this teaching will strengthen the Spirit as a consequence of a respectful and intentional behavior.

✑

"The priority is to be the person that I like, rather than trying to be a person that others like."
~Heather

✑

3

DUALITY

Duality is an important topic in which seekers of truth have been contemplating upon extensively. Many people, in an attempt to clarify the concept of duality by simplifying it, have inadvertently complicated it and the have made the process of understanding it more obscure. This error has been done mostly by avoiding to make distinctions between the different types of dualities.

This simplification has been in describing all dualities as opposites while using approximation to make sense of it in a very abstract way. We believe that there are certainly exceptions to the rule but, for the most part, dualities can be divided in: Opposites and Complementary forms of duality. The distinction between these two is very important:

Good and Bad are opposites.
Male and Female are complementary.

The fact that something has an opposite, however, does not automatically mean that the opposite must be kept in regard and honored as a deserving necessity. A common teaching that we have come across in the New-Age Spiritual world is that humans need "bad" to understand "good"; and, therefore they need them both to exist. We do not know for sure if the absence of the understanding of "bad" would compromise our capacity to enjoy "good", but we certainly do not believe that being exposed to "bad" is in any way something necessary for us and for seekers of truth. Imagine an evolved future we could all have where "bad and evil" were merely obsolete words mentioned in the encyclopedia just to remind us of how brilliant we were to get rid of it and constrict those concepts to the smallest of forms... a mentioned word.

Diversity is an aspect of duality that we acknowledge. And we have found two main mind-sets deeply rooted within Human Beings in regards to diversity. Both can result in profound unbalanced, nonobjective and unpleasant, but likely, scenarios. One mindset believes that the best and easiest way to deal with diversity is by eliminating it altogether when it is somewhat of an obstacle. The other mindset is characterized by ignoring all the negative aspects of everything and defending those negative aspects simply for the sake of honoring diversity.

We believe that diversity should be acknowledged, understood, and then handled as Intentional Beings ought to do with all things. Which means: honor, uphold, and expand all that carries beauty, goodness, constructive teachings, and all kinds of positive attributes. The negative aspects that remain should then be recognized, acknowledged to be nonconstructive and counterproductive towards positive outcomes, and therefore, not honored nor upheld. The negative aspects can now be rejected, isolated, and analyzed from time to time in the future, in case new information brings up a different positive prospective over them.

Recently we met someone who was trying to gently compel us into the mentality that we, as humans, are really not much more than brute beasts who react to situations based on their domestication and brute instincts. The person asked Gio, "what would you do if someone was bad-mouthing Heather?"

Gio replied, "I am a Being deeply committed to be an Intentional Being. Therefore, rather than answering what I may do if I would let my instincts and my domestications overtake me, I will tell you what an Intentional Being would do. An Intentional Being would question whether a RE-action would be the result of the teachings that they have received, or whether it is the beast instinct that one may be submitting to by RE-acting. Once having been amused by which of the two would create the primitive boost for a RE-action, an Intentional Being would take charge of self, rather than RE-acting. They would then consider what response would likely generate the most constructive outcome for the sake of the beloved one, the person doing the bad-mouthing, and for the rest of the Universe... Even the Universe will learn, because of the fact that we are all connected, a constructive lesson from such an impeccable and intentional behavior."

The reason this story is being mentioned, however, is not only for educational purposes on how an Intentional Being ought to behave. An Intentional Being balances the positive aspects of masculine and feminine traits in order to avoid confrontation whenever possible and transform a challenging negative situation into a constructive source for teaching and learning for all involved. The reason why this story is being mentioned is to identify the most common RE-actions which humans are domesticated to display which represent the negative masculine and the negative feminine. When a subject who is dominated by a negative masculine trait is confronted, they will portray their negative masculine with an overly aggressive confrontational RE-action. When a person dominated by a negative feminine trait is confronted, they will portray their negative feminine by shutting down and purposely avoiding any kind of confrontation altogether. This includes also the kinds of confrontations that are often necessary in order for opinions and ideas to be exchanged, and by doing so, replacing the mystifying assumptions that result from a lack of communication with facts and opinions. Some refer to these RE-actions as the equivalent of having a metaphorical button that gets pushed and gives way to an automatic response. The fact is that we are not machines with buttons and whether or not we decide that we are slaves to a program for which an automatic outburst is the direct result of a button being pushed is entirely up to us.

꒜

Re-actions are usually the responses to actions which we ourselves have witnessed and now find ourselves re-enacting.

꒜

Some modern humans understand the concept that there is a masculine and a feminine aspect within each and every person, regardless of their gender. That is the first step towards understanding the true nature of humans, since in the past males were encouraged only to acknowledge their masculine aspects, and females their feminine ones. Now that this dual nature can be easily acknowledged, it is time to double that and start envisioning a quad nature. This quad nature creates four aspects: Positive Feminine, Negative Feminine, Positive Masculine, and Negative Masculine[10]. The quad model offers not only a better understanding, but also the tools for becoming better Beings. After acknowledging, studying, and gaining an understanding of these four aspects, one can then weed out the negative aspects and focus on the positive contributions in order to become a better person.

---

10 For further exploration of this concept, we recommend a book called *Four Faces in the Mirror*, By Vito Hemphill.

Positive Feminine	Positive Masculine
Negative Feminine	Negative Masculine

The lesson that many Spiritual teachers are currently professing which states to balance the masculine and the feminine is incomplete, for two reasons. The first reason is within the fact that balancing implies that all genders are required to find the balance by implementing equal amounts of feminine and masculine character traits. Being in touch with both aspects, however, does not mean that we all are required to find our comfort zone in the same 50/50 ratio, but we become aware of the existence of this dual nature and become able to tune ourselves into both of them at will for the sake of obtaining the best results in everything that we do. The second reason for which we have found these simplistic teachings to be incomplete is that the only objective way that this process of balancing becomes constructive is when it consists of acknowledging that there are certain specific traits that can be classified as negative traits within the masculine and within the feminine. These traits tend to be protected by the habitual way of humans to deal with those things that may be considered offensive: For the sake of avoiding to offend those who over-identify with the masculine and/or the feminine traits, humans accept and purposely ignore and avoid to methodically single out all the negative aspects and avoid to act as intentional, objective, constructive, courageous Beings and focus on getting rid of or isolating and minimizing their negative effects. This process is what transforms a generic concept (which may cause one to feel good, but lacks constructivism) into a real method which honors the positive masculine and the positive feminine. This process allows the result of deep honoring to become an act of profound voluntary change.

For ages humans have attempted to find the balance in the masculine and feminine realms. They have identified themselves so much in either of these groups and have forgotten that the priority for them to be part of either of these groups was to protect or to defend **only** the positive aspects of these groups and shed the negative traits by learning how magnificently the combination of positive aspects of both unite. The positive aspects of these two, **because** they are complementary, do not necessitate the negative aspects of either. They can utilize the much more balanced mechanisms woven within their positive aspects to produce actions which are more likely to succeed in producing the best results.

Both masculine and feminine negative traits are deeply rooted within Human Beings; the unfortunate assumption, by many, is that all traits within human nature have to be preserved. The good news is that this is not so. Humans will retain (if it serves them) their masculinity and/or their femininity even if they let go of the negative aspects of both. Humans' identification with one or the other can be upheld if necessary, by holding onto only the positive sides of both. Masculine and Feminine manifest two different forms of energy that we are all somewhat familiar with. We believe that the balancing between the two and the deep understanding of both is the key, as opposed to the suppression of either.

We have researched the beliefs and explanations from many different groups of Spiritual Seekers who have existed and built upon these beliefs for thousands of years, including Shamans, Yogis, New-Agers, ourselves and others. It is our conclusion that females are generally more tuned-in and at ease with their intuitive capacities while males tend to be more tuned-in and at ease with their rational self. These differences are so pronounced that many times it makes both sexes incapable of really communicating and understanding each other. This is much more than a statement based on perception but a process of research and analyzation that we have been focused on for a long time.

Other forms of complementary manifestations of the masculine and feminine include Yin and Yang, front and back, and defensive and offensive. The

feminine aspects tends to be defensive, and the masculine tends to be offensive. It is for this reason that in Eastern Medicine the front of the body is considered Yang, or masculine and the back of the body is Yin or feminine. The Tao or "Yin Yang" symbol represents the complementary nature of the Masculine and the Feminine. Neither one can exist without the other.

These differences are gifts, which serve each of the two categories, but can also keep them apart unless they are able to share their gifts with each other. Evolved feminine capacities, which are often but not exclusively prevalent in females, are so mystical and pronounced that they are often perceived, by those who are not in touch with the same capacities which are often males, as threats and isolated as defects rather than gifts. Some have developed their feminine capacity of perceiving subtle energies to such a degree that it is incomprehensible to those who have not.

Those who have been gifted with evolved masculine capacities have actually a gift and perhaps a burden to follow a path based on objective rationalization. They do not have, in general, the capacities to perceive energies with the same ease as their feminine counterparts. Nor do they feel comfortable dwelling in an abstract understanding and explanation of things. This too is a gift and a burden as it forces them to look for an understanding of things based on an accumulation of facts and processed information. It is extremely important, while understanding the benefits of acknowledging and balancing both the masculine and the feminine characteristics that either of the two are found within both genders and often they are mastered, and brought to a new level, by the complementary gender. The founder of Objectivism, which is the name of the movement that holds the dominance of reason over all other forms of processing information, Ayn Rand, is a brilliant female philosopher. She accomplished to create a movement for which reason is not based on ones preferences, but on reality.

For thousands of years, lead by Religious rule, humans would offer their beliefs as a legitimate alternative to reason and demand for reason to bow to their beliefs despite rationality. Ayn Rand's philosophy focuses on the potential greatness within the human brain rather than the view of humans merely as powerless followers of wishful thinking. She has brought a great contribution to the seek for Intentional Conscious Evolution and appreciation of the potential of the human race as Objective Beings. She was exposed to an aspect of Religious followers who empowered the idea that humans are, by nature, lesser Beings whose destiny relies either on external forces, or on an uncompromising avoidance of reality.

Spirituality is not the opposite of objectivity. In its purest form, objectivity is the necessary and empowering complement of an Evolved Being who is able to align their capacity of living truth, which is the impeccable result of cross-referencing truth with objective reasoning, with their intuitive insights. There is no question that the commonly misused and misleading understanding of compassion[11] has often defied or not acknowledged truth and objectivism. There is also no doubt, however, that **real** compassion needs to be an essential ingredient in the formula that

---

11 See: Ch. 15, Compassion, pg. 116

relies on rationality and maintains the objective of producing the best results in order to advance humanity towards being more Evolved Beings who honor the result derived from conscious productivity, and also honor the Compassionate Being within.

"Man has a single basic choice: to think or not, and that is the gauge of his virtue. Moral perfection is an unbreached rationality— not the degree of your intelligence, but the full and relentless use of your mind, not the extent of your knowledge, but the acceptance of reason as an absolute."[12]

---

12 From Galt's Speech, *Atlas Shrugged* - Ayn Rand

4

GOOD vs. EVIL

Whether we choose it or not, we are all active participants in the ongoing battle between good and evil. Each one of us is faced, during this physical journey, with choices that involve us, and choices that involve others. As we evolve Spiritually, we become aware that very rarely the choices that we believe regard only us do not effect other Beings— perhaps even never. Being good means to prioritize the search for the awareness of how and where this connection with others exists in each of the choices we make, and choosing to do the right thing each time.

"There is no truth", "there is no right or wrong", and "there is no good or bad" are all resulting from the same mechanism. This is the reaction to the past millennial of extreme unquestionable, and unchangeable patriarchal doctrines. The correct path does not require one to adopt yet another extreme; on the contrary, the correct path is one of moderation and equilibrium. A balance of the heart and the mind. As long as there is good action, good will continue to exist, and as long as there is evil action, evil will continue to exist. The Spiritual Path brings one to the exploration and dedication to what is good.

There is a commonly spread rumor that good and evil need to co-exist or that good and bad are only relative to interpretation. This implication is not keeping into consideration, however, the most important aspect of our decision making: *intentions*. When one searches, with an open loving heart and an open rational mind, for the highest good of all involved, their intentions are good. We can absolutely conceive of a world where the concept of bad is understood, yet there is no demonstration of it in order for us to appreciate the good... A world where all Beings live in a constant state of consideration for others and make a point to seek the truth and do the right thing. This is the world that we are trying to create.

The Manual of Spiritual Living is about evolving Spiritually in order to do what is good and doing what is good in order to evolve Spiritually. That is because doing what is good enhances ones Spiritual Evolution, and enhancing our Spiritual Evolution brings one to do what is good. We feel that the concept for which "there is no good or bad" is a denial that we are responsible for our actions and for the consequences of these actions. The comfort zone that is created by such a concept is elusive and prevents us from acknowledging that we are the people in charge, and this being in charge is that which makes us Evolving Spiritual Beings.

This means that we are equally responsible for the actions that we take as much as we are responsible for the times in which we choose not to take action. Everything we do, or choose not to do, matters.

"Ignorance is bliss"— we have all probably heard this phrase at one time or another, and perhaps related to it in some way. Many people confuse being good with acting as if they were good, while they purposely embrace the ignorance and refuse to acknowledge the available information when making choices. We believe we owe it to ourselves and others to always **see the world for what it is, rather than the way we wish for it to be.** This is also fundamental for real co-creation to occur[13]. When we neglect to acknowledge the truth we are not being good; instead, we are sacrificing good in exchange for a more comfortable illusion which may harm ourselves and others as a consequence of such an irresponsible and selfish behavior.

Wishful thinking is a beautiful way to imagine truth the way we wish for it to be. It should inspire us to prepare the grounds for that reality to come forth. This can only be achieved, however, by combining ones hopeful vision with the acknowledgment of the facts. Then, we may use our rational mind to examine which steps will hopefully take us, one day, towards our imagined reality. Avoiding to face facts in a rational way means taking steps in the wrong direction. An Awakened Spiritual Seeker can see through the dogmas which are meant to prevent us from seeing the truth.

13 See: Ch. 21, Manifestation, pg. 154

Those dogmas are there only to smooth up the edges and create a seemingly comfortable zone, where truth is denied access.

All of us, at all times, are either part of the solution or part of the problem. It is our constant choices which will move us in one direction or the other. Choosing to be part of the solution is a clear statement that we are, in fact, choosing what we believe to be "good" which, as consequence, means we acknowledge the existence of "good and bad" and our awareness of it.

Making choices is not a choice.

We are constantly choosing what we are doing in the present and what to do next. Whether we acknowledge it or not, each and every choice we make is leaning towards good or leaning towards bad. What remains up to us is the consciousness behind each of these choices. The fear of doing wrong is shared by all humans, to some extent, who care about the consequences derived by their choices, whether they are conscious about it, or not. Courage is not the absence of fear, it is the act of reacting to fear and prioritizing what we believe is right over our instinct to flee. While trying to do what is good we risk to be wrong and do what is not good; however, that should not be a deterrent to seek what is good, but rather an ulterior boost for us to question our motives, information, and goals.

5

FEAR

Humans have made fear another victim of their attempt to simplify everything. People often attribute two driving forces behind all human behavior, one being love and the other being fear. Love is considered, by these same people, to be the opposite of fear. It is in this scenario that humans are given two choices, one in which they behave out of love, and the other in which they behave out of fear. This simplistic way of thinking has often been responsible for making things more complicated by focusing more on the act of the simplification process rather than making things accurate. Many of the situations that Human Beings are exposed to are complicated and it takes a more complicated formula to understand them. The teachings of this book are trying to reach humans on an intellectual level that focuses on accuracy rather than the simplicity that has been adopted by the mainstream. The priority is that the formulas are correct, not simple, otherwise they become meaning-less and can create even more confusion.

While our experience has taught us that love is the ultimate driving force on the Spiritual path, objective reasoning has taught us that fear is not the opposite of love. As far as we are aware, love has no opposite, because it is the ultimate state of being for humans at their current level of evolution.

It is not constructive to fear fear. The opposite of the feeling of fear is simply a positive anxious anticipation where one looks forward for something joyful to occur. Fear can also be beneficial, as it can help to keep us from harm. Fear is the message that the body gives to the brain to alert a person of potential harm. It is also both possible and common to love and to have fears at the same time. Just because one is full of love does not mean that they are absent of fear. Many times being full of love, and having many loved ones, gives one *more* reasons to fear. Managing and understanding what fear is and how to benefit from it, rather than be a slave to it, brings about heightened awareness and allows one not to dwell in a place of fear.

The more humankind evolves, and the more their love expands. The more their love expands, and the more Beings become part of a love circle. The more Beings there are within a love circle, the more the possibilities that something can happen to one or more of them. So, in a sense, Spiritual Evolution can give you even more reasons to fear. Many contemporary teachings teach one to avoid fear altogether, and this can be confusing. A more constructive and complete way to express what these teachings are trying to express would be:

When confronted with fear, act courageously.

Courage is the act of bringing awareness to fearful possible upcoming events and dealing with them. Courage is not the absence of fear, but rather a constructive attitude to confront the fear.

Many humans walking on a Spiritual Path have occasionally accessed their connection to their higher intuition[14]; and, as a consequence have immediately felt a sense of release coming from knowing that they have nothing to worry about. These events brought them immediate awareness of a connection with a Higher Knowledge. Many of these people have also spread the message that all humans have, at all times, the capacity to access this information themselves. This "discovery" of having access to a higher and shared accessible knowledge has also led them to believe that humans have nothing to fear. This is a beautiful concept, however we believe it is only partially true. The idea that ALL humans have the possibility to access the information of the Collective Consciousness is a

---

14 See: Chapter 25, Intuition, pg. 182

possibility. This means that we too consider this capacity may be accessible to ALL, but we are also aware of the lack of integrity that humans tend to have when attempting to be completely truthful. They often confuse the information they have received by tuning into the Collective Consciousness with the creation of their own wishful thinking[15]. We do not know whether all humans have reached the stage of evolution or have developed their capacity to intentionally or randomly unintentionally access the higher knowledge. Also we do not know, nor assume, that the comforting message that is often received for which "there is nothing to fear" is in regards to all events, or rather to one event in particular.

Fear can, and often does, become overwhelming to the point in which the decisions that arise are not the conscious decisions that the higher self would make. This often leads to a less-than-impeccable behavior. Dwelling in fear is not wise nor productive and often people shift from overindulging in it to ignoring it all together. For these reasons, it is important to learn how to confront and deal with fear.

The feeling of fear can be intentionally managed to serve us in a positive way. There are some motives that can be honored and for which fear can be a useful tool to serve our higher self, and other motives for which fear must be overcome. A fear that is commonly overruled by the ego is on whether or not one is liked by other people. This is understandable, but we have to strive to be the best we can for ourselves. If this is what

---

15 See: Chapter 21, Manifestation, pg. 154

we are doing in an impeccable way, then we will like ourselves for real and whether other people are able to see the intentionality and the impeccability behind all of our doings will determine whether they are worthy of our liking. Indulging in self-pity over other people liking us when we have, and we are, doing our part as Intentional Beings, belongs to the part of fears that we do not want to honor.

Preparing as best as possible for the future, thanks to fear, is an act of courage. Ignoring the future is an attempt to cowardly avoid unpleasant situations that could have been foreseen, and perhaps prevented or even transformed into something beautiful for all. Many people live by the premise that a peaceful state of mind requires being in the present without worrying about the future. While there is some truth to this, in order to avoid having to worry about the future, many times one must first take steps in order to make that happen.

Many teachings today advise humans to live in the Now[16]. Living in the Now is a great concept, as the meaning of it is about being present in the moment that we are living, as opposed to being absent while thinking always about what to do next. At the same time, it is important to balance the act of living in the Now with the awareness of what the future holds. The correct way of bringing balance to the act of living in the Now is by being present yet aware that the future is the consequence of the Now. Living in the Now is an evolving state of being, and as such, it is important to

---

16 See: Chapter 18, Awareness... Be here Now, Pg. 135

cultivate such a state. Doing so properly, however, necessitates a balance between indulging in a peaceful present time and creating the basis for a peaceful future tomorrow.

It is important to live in the present moment, but it is also important to maintain the awareness that the present moment will change and the future is more than a mere mental construct on this physical plane. If someone is lost in the woods, and they know that it will be getting cold, it is the fear of the unpleasant feeling of cold that acts as a catalyst for action. We recommend refraining from becoming enslaved by this fear, but we also recommend to recognize it as one of the forces which pushes us to prevent an unpleasant situation. In this case, by reminding one to go to collect some wood and therefore, be able to make a fire and avoid the unpleasant feeling of being cold. It is the fear of being burned that will remind us that the fire we will light that night can burn us and it is up to us to surround it with rocks to prevent it from spreading. In other words, do not harvest the fear but **harvest the solutions to all preventable situations which fear has helped you to become aware of in the Now.**

Some Beings are blessed with a peaceful present, while others are not. Becoming aware of other people's suffering means to start the process which enables one to become a partial contributor to the solutions which will alleviate or heal their suffering. It is our acquaintance with the suffering of others that inspires us to be part of the solution. The amount of involvement that one decides to dedicate to helping others may vary. We have found that helping others is part of evolving, as the Collective Consciousness includes all of us and when others evolve we do too, because of that collectiveness. Most importantly, it is the right thing to do. We all are living different existences and we all have different situations. Overextending our contribution can be just as damaging to us as being aloof and indifferent. At the same time, remaining comfortably wrapped in a bubble of self-absorption, despite the suffering of others, is the opposite behavior of that of a truly compassionate Being. One would progress by becoming aware of the fact that existing is not the only contribution one has to offer. At the same time, it is important to keep in mind that it is not correct to sacrifice all of ones existence in the name of contribution. Finding ones balance between over involvement and lack of involvement, depending on the issue, is the preferable course of action.

Humans react differently to different types of fear. We have observed that the Negative Masculine[17] human aspect tends to indulge in fear. It may over-react by confronting a danger before it is actually dangerous. This behavior is often criticized by those who are coming from a more Feminine approach, who often claim that wars are the consequence of a male-dominated society. This perspective tends to say that if women were to rule the world, there would be no wars. However, a Negative Feminine aspect also exists, which does everything to avoid the feeling of fear all together.

17 See: Chapter 3, Duality... Positive Masculine, Positive Feminine, Negative Masculine, Negative Feminine, pg. 37

This aspect does its best to avoid acknowledging any of the negative consequences that arise from in-action, even when a threat is apparent and undeniable.

A balanced Positive Masculine and Positive Feminine approach creates both a complementary and a constructive attitude. Fear derived from imminent dangers is acknowledged and the reactions to the consequences are met with truly compassionate actions. Elimination of imminent dangers can be a compassionate act, as the killing of a rattlesnake next to a child could be, when no other option is available. Keeping in mind that our goal, as Spiritual Beings, is to tune ourselves into the Universe and the Collective Consciousness to the point where we could communicate with the snake and know whether or not the child was in any danger. However, the danger assessment must be the result of impeccable objective reasoning combined with open hearted intuition, and never the result of wishful thinking[18].

Awakening Spiritually means extending ones awareness. Currently humankind is doing less than wonderful things around the Earth; and, it is important to extend ones awareness outside of ones close vicinity. Just as the butterfly beating its wings in China effects life in the USA, so does the suffering and death of other Beings. Becoming aware, as opposed to being aloof, about what is hidden behind religious, cultural, and territorial boundaries is a duty of every member of the human family. It is in no way an act of love to ignore what is going on and by doing so, validating the

------

18 See: Ch. 21, Manifestation, pg. 154

horrendous racism toward women, men, and animals around the world. It is an act of cowardice masqueraded as tolerance. Too much of what is happening becomes suppressed by those who claim they do not want to spread fear, but in reality are engulfed by it. It is not fear that motivates many to act toward spreading the awareness, it is courage and noble intentions. If the knowledge of what is happening brings up an emotion of fear, simply act courageously.

"The world will not be destroyed by those who do evil, but by those who watch them without doing anything." ~ Albert Einstein

6

SHEDDING THE LAYERS

The concept of *"shedding the layers"* has been around for a long time, but few have attempted to elaborate it in a way that could be understood and practiced. The concept is about looking within to find the real self, God/Goddess, all answers, peace, freedom, happiness, truth, and more. This concept is somewhat challenging to comprehend and deeply challenging to put into practice— especially for those people who rely mostly on a linear way of thinking. Many probably picture themselves meditating with their eyes closed trying to find all these things which one is supposed to be able to find within, but finding themselves being overwhelmed by inner chatter. Others may simply get bored or sleepy. Most people however, will likely begin to meditate on the image of themselves that they have obtained as a result of what other people have created for them and attempt either to be that which others see them to be or attempt to change their image in the eyes of others by creating an alternative profile for the self.

As a result of these attempts to decipher the self, rather than focusing on finding who they are, Human Beings create several layers of who they were and continually add more layers to this creation. Often, they are so unaware of these layers that they believe life experiences and their learning from these experiences are the only things influencing who they have become. For example, if one goes out of the house and gets hit by a bicycle, and believes that the experience of getting hit by a bicycle makes them who they are, they are missing the point. They are the person who gave an interpretation to the meaning of being hit by the bicycle and chose a course of action accordingly. In other words, whether following the experience they chose to stay home in order to avoid bicycles, or to become a biker, or to be more alert about bicycles, or to invent a bicycle which would not hurt when hitting someone and make themselves rich, it is their decision in response to the experience which is going to influence who they become.

Very often when pain is experienced people choose to avoid situations which put them at risk of experiencing more of it; and, they keep their memories of their life's lessons vivid in an attempt to avoid getting hurt again in the future. While avoiding pain is a wise course of action, one does not have to allow it to define who they are, and if one carries vivid layers of past pain they may end up shadowing who they are today. The truth is that this state of mind should be overcome by an intentional choice to transcend this acceptance of being a result of the events and become an Intentional Being who treasures experiences and life lessons but does not identify themselves as the end result of these. Once the concept of shedding the layers is generally understood, what remains is to understand how to go about doing it.

Generally speaking, people's understanding of who they are consists of the rational identification they have constructed of themselves. This rational interpretation is based on the information available and the comparison that they make between themselves and others. The world is divided into countless groups, religions, races, nationalities, ethnic groups, and more. Many humans make it their priority to defend all of the groups they believe themselves to belong to. Many teachings that have spread within all of these groups are focused on making each member of the group proud to belong to it. They teach others to devote themselves to the group and to defend the group.

This division is not based on who people are, nor on who their enlightened selves would want them to be and become. It has little or nothing to do with who one is and who one can become— it is only who they have been convinced and accepted to be stuck upon being. Whatever is the thing that we grew up feeling and believing to be a part of us is questioned by the Intentional Spiritual Seeker who seeks the truth. Question everything and be impeccable when objectively discerning what you want to hang onto and what you need to let go of. Whichever country one is born in is likely to have a reputation for different things, some good and some bad. If one can be proud only for the good things, and one is impeccable in their judgement, then they realize that it is not the country where they were born and where they grew up that they have to be proud of, but only what good comes from those teachings. The same process of thought can be applied to race, religion, sex, culture, or any other group that one affiliates with. This is one of the main ways to remove the layers that have been fabricated around our intentional self.

Truth is the most important tool that we have for finding out other truths. Many humans have a habit of approximation when dealing with the truth. The amount of truth that they themselves express is usually less than impeccable. We have learned how being true in our judgements, being true in our answers, being true in every single detail in each and every story we tell, and motives behind any result we want to achieve, is the most effective way to shed layers. We are aware, however, it is an extremely tedious and long process to reach such an impeccable layer of truthfulness.

When one is able to be true to themselves and true to others they may expose a side of themselves that they were unknowingly keeping secret. They were keeping it secret from others, and often from themselves in an attempt to protect themselves. Many times, during our own Spiritual Journey, we expected that the consequences of applying the concept of being impeccable with telling and living the truth would have been extremely painful and perhaps even altogether devastating. Instead, **truth seems to have its own private access to the light regardless of how deep it**

is buried within of us. In our experiences, it has been the most cleansing process ever. It has been incredible how the consequences of consistently telling the truth defy our rational, yet pessimistic expectations and when the veils of deceit are removed the light which comes through sets us up for a new beautiful and unpredictable outcome.

The light that comes in while shedding these layers becomes part of who we are. We feel lighter as a consequence of the energy which is released, trapped within these layers upon layers. We feel ourselves becoming of more light as we perceive this light reaching our core and becoming part of who we are. This is an ongoing process and the visual perception of layers wrapped around us becomes clearer and even more obvious with the more layers we are able to peel off of us. What also becomes easier to perceive is that there are many more layers to us than we would have previously been able to understand, see, or comprehend without having started from the outermost layers. Those are usually the hardest to remove.

Our physical body is made of tiny vibrating particles. The feeling that results from shedding the layers and letting more and more light access, fuel, and reach us will eventually create the distinct feeling that we can feel and perceive the vibrations of these particles. We are setting up for becoming capable of reaching the full awareness, instinctive and rational, that we are those vibrating particles and those vibrating particles are effected by who we choose to be.

We believe that soon will come the day in which the ability to intervene directly with the vibration of the molecules of the physical body and the physical Universe will be accessible to an increasing number of humans. The time for this, for obvious safety reasons, will come when humans are evolved enough that their intentional impact concerning the manipulations of these vibrations will be led by an utmost impeccable and intentional behavior. If this was not so, the results of such an evolutionary leap could be catastrophic. When humans will be able, in a significant number, to align their intentions with the highest good, which we believe the Universe is already aware of, then our co-creating capacities will be able to manifest themselves to the fullest. This is not a process of wishful thinking—it is the result of an objective process of deductive reasoning.

The act referred to as *"raising the vibration"* is much less mystical and much easier to achieve now that it has been given a rational explanation of what the vibration is referring to. And it is not pretentious to believe that if we are capable of tuning into the vibrating particles that we are made of, then we can directly effect this vibration and therefore, be the Intentional Beings who can raise their own vibrations.

7

FITTING A PROFILE

This is probably one of the most important aspects of human behavior that necessitates a deeper understanding at this point in human history. Author Eckhart Tolle has done a wonderful job in expressing the tendency of our ego to find an identity for itself. He wisely explains that we are not our ego, in fact, the ego is merely a part of who we are. The ego part of us relies entirely on a rational, mental construct of who we are. Because we are ever-changing Beings, our true self can never be entirely bounded by this mental construct.

We are actually the consciousness which oversees the ego's boundaries and keeps destroying them in order to expand those bounds and encompass our true nature, which is boundless.

Once we have established that our true self does not need, nor desires, to be restrained within a mental construct, our duty becomes to recognize the boundaries and the profiles created within us. Then, we must climb the ladder to continue our ongoing Spiritual Evolution as if each and every profile that we found ourselves impersonating throughout our life was a step on an infinite ladder. We may want to acknowledge and be grateful for our capacity for creating these mental constructs of who we are as they can be useful, but above all, we want to focus our awareness in never letting them interfere with our process of becoming.

Artistic plays and movies throughout human history have continuously created, elaborated, and portrayed new human profiles. This has been beneficial in many ways, as more and more people were able to find a profile to identify with, and by doing so they shared the pleasurable feeling of fitting into this world. Thanks to technology and the fact that our means of communication have increased, each profile identity has been elaborated and many more profile identities have been created that never existed before. Unsurprisingly, many more profiles will be identified as the human race as a whole proceeds to evolve.

Imagine a profile as a costume: you find it, you like it, you wear it, you show it around and you enjoy it for the time being, knowing that eventually it will not suit you anymore. During ones Spiritual Journey teachings will continually be received, and if one constantly allows oneself to learn from these teachings, one will also allow oneself to change accordingly from these new perspectives. Simultaneously, ones view of oneself will change. The changes that take place in the consciousness are profound during this journey; but, it will depend on us how fast and how far we are willing to evolve. The more layers of costumes that we will peal off of us, and the more we will be free to expand our awareness without the constrictions of any unnecessary costume whatsoever. The costumes one wears will eventually feel obsolete. There is no finite costume that one ought to wear, like one of a Divine Being, Guru, Spiritual leader or a Saint. Simply allow oneself to be, in each moment, the Being one wishes to be.

Many Spiritual Seekers are often seduced into fitting the Guru-Devotee profile, as either a guru or a devotee. We strongly discourage this, as it is truly a distraction on the path to becoming what we truly are. Masquerading as an enlightened person and being one are very different, and in the modern society few people are able to discern the difference. When one is impeccable about their motives in everything they do, there is no worry about this because doing something in order to fit a profile is a less than impeccable motive, even when it is others, and not ourselves that have created that profile.

Be aware, for the profiles we wear always feel as if we are actually them. These profiles will not feel like a costume, but rather as our own skin. The longer one wears their profiles, and the more they feel as if the profiles are the essence of who they are. It takes a huge amount of courage and determination to even consider the possibility that the constructed profile IS merely a self-made costume. Only after we successfully peel off the profile will it become evident to us that we are more whole without the costume, than while wearing it.

"The self-confidence of the warrior is not the self-confidence of the average man. The average man seeks certainty in the eyes of the onlooker and calls that self-confidence. The warrior seeks impeccability in his own eyes and calls that humbleness. The average man is hooked to his fellow men, while the warrior is hooked only to infinity." ~ Castenada

8

THE EMPEROR'S NEW CLOTHES

Many Humans Beings grow up looking for a part to impersonate which seems to fit them and reflects the way they would like other people to see them. One struggles to achieve this while people around them contribute with their interpretation of who one is. The role playing tends to become a huge part of one's existence. There are times in which, even after many years of changing roles, all it takes is running into a person from the past and that encounter is enough to trigger a Re-action for which one starts to play the role that one used to play in their shared past with this person. Family roles are some of the most entrapping and the ones which people tend to fall back into the most easily.

Spiritual Seekers, who honor their seek above all, may find themselves renouncing to participate in wearing a profile as part of their commitment to their unconfined path. In other words, they will not cherish and accept to behave within any boundaries of role playing and in each moment they will behave in accordance with their commitment to being who they choose to be rather than complying with the expectations of others.

Noncompliance with wearing a designated costume in order to fit a profile represents a new and even more intense challenge: The less costumes one wears and the more difficult it is for one to be accepted by others, who naturally tend to want them to fit them into a character that they can recognize and play along with. People are so used to everyone wearing some form of costume, that they will literally see all others wearing one, even when there is none to be seen. This is like the children's book, *The Emperor's New Clothes*. Not wearing a profile is confusing to people around us because they are busy playing their part and do not know how to interact with us if they do not understand which character we are meant to play.

We have encountered many Spiritual Seekers during our ongoing Spiritual Journey. As our knowledge and understanding of the Spiritual realm grew, so did the expectations of people around us to identify us with the well-defined profiles within their construct of a Spiritual teacher or leader. It has been an intense and challenging task for us to constantly avoid falling into the trap of fitting the ultimate profile for a New-Age Spiritual Seeker. It also took quite a bit of sense of humor, to de-mystify our "Guru-ness" and be impeccable about our commitment to evolution, free of all unnecessary boundaries.

Identification into a well defined profile or character is very tempting. It also takes dedication and focus to realize how the profile that we have in mind is the result of a series of other peoples ideas of that profile which comes to us from the surrounding information. The widely known common image of the Guru immediately brings one to think of all those people who have been defined as Gurus. The mind immediately thinks of the faces of the known, or so called Gurus of the time period we are living in, or from the past. During the 20th Century that would mean.... the Dalai Lama, Yoda (from Star Wars), The Karate Kid master, and then depending on ones involvement with the world of the Spiritual Gurus the list of names would grow into Sai Baba, Osho, Yogi Bhajan, YogaAnanda, Amma, and many more. Immediately after having these images passing into ones mind also characteristics of their behavior will appear and what the Guru-type has in common. By association, one may then begin mimicking that learned behavior. In the case of the Spiritual Guru's behavior, one would feel compelled to refrain from showing emotions and remain constantly in a state of perceivable dis-attachment from the lower emotional states in which most humans tend to indulge. One may also be tempted to be the visible example, wearing loose clothing, beads, and a very Eastern attire. The Guru image generally portrays an attitude for which it is possible to have all of the answers and if everybody only knew what they knew, then they would know there was nothing to worry about. It is actually that attitude that helped us to see that we, personally, did not want to be part of the Guru mentality. What we believe, is that more importantly than having others trust that we have all the answers, we should actually become aware, and take responsibility for the fact that the world is not perfect and there could be much more Spiritual Evolution taking place. This means that maybe all these Gurus do not have all the answers and there are many more answers needed in order to continuously make this world into a better place.

We treasure the importance of sharing impeccable truths as part of what is helping us to evolve and find more answers through Spiritual Evolution. What is even more important though, is that if we can surround ourselves with other impeccable seekers of truth whose desire is not to follow us, but instead to co-lead with us, then it seems very probable that better results would be obtained faster. A world of Gurus all co-leading one another and sharing an impeccable commitment to find all truths sounds much more appealing to us than a world divided by Gurus and devotees. At a certain point of our Spiritual Seek we realized that there were not Gurus available to us that reflected entirely or were aligned with our Spiritual Awakenings. This is when we knew we were in total absence of a model to impersonate, and we had to abandon the enticing perspective of following a pre-paved path and a pre-conceived Guru stereotype.

The commitment to our impeccability is the force we choose to honor, even when we become aware that the people around us may get confused from the impossibility for them to place us in one of their collected profile images. For this reason, we adopted to use only a non-model of constructed profiles and instead each moment we truly use our best efforts to be impeccable in trying to be who we want to become. The commitment of a Spiritual Evolutionist is to reinvent themselves constantly in accordance to what represents the highest image of Goodness they can conceive of.

9

GURUNESS

Dictionary.com defines a Guru as any person who teaches or advises. A common usage for the word Guru describes a physical being who has evolved their awareness and understanding of the Spiritual realm and has chosen to teach their path. Many of these Beings believe they have reached a level of evolution that allows them to see the human realm from a higher prospective and have chosen to teach in this lifetime, dedicating themselves to facilitate others on their paths.

We, like many Spiritual Seekers, have spent a significant portion of our Spiritual search on finding a Guru or a Spiritual teacher who would not only reflect the conclusions that we have reached, but that would be in a much more advanced stage of understanding these Spiritual conclusions and who would be as impeccable as we are in not letting anything stall their Spiritual growth and their commitment to continuously evolve and perhaps even share tools for all Beings to participate in the evolutionary process. As yet, we have not found such a Being except in each other. Although we have encountered several Spiritual teachers and Spiritual Seekers whom are extremely powerful from an energetic and evolutionary perspective, we have not yet found anybody more advanced in their all-around Spiritual development than one another. We have been each others Gurus and acknowledge our union and our exchange of energy and information as the greatest source yet of rational, objective, and Spiritual knowledge.

A common belief of Spiritual Seekers is that intuition, in truth, is the real viewing tool which allows humans to see through a veil. The veil is commonly referred to as the "veil of illusion" or "maya". This belief entails that the veil has been created to prevent humans from experiencing their physical journey to the fullest, and only when ready, do humans gain the Spiritual Evolution required for breaking through this veil. Like the butterfly, humans must gain their strength by struggling to break through the cocoon that veils them from the other side of the known reality. A Spiritual Guru supposedly has the capacity to see through this veil. One word that may define this capacity is Enlightenment, as this veil is also viewed as a divider or curtain in between us and the light of 'God'. God being the source of all available shared knowledge to which Spiritually Evolved Beings can connect and become a part of God.

Once a sought-out Guru has been found, many Spiritual Seekers dedicate an important part of their time in following the Guru. They look for someone who will teach them to awaken their understanding of their Spiritual Self and guide them through this process. Most Spiritual Seekers consider Spiritual Evolution a process which needs to be taken upon as a solo-journey or by following the doctrine of a "Spiritual Guru" who doesn't require, nor expects them, to reach their level of Spiritual Evolution, but rather expects them to dwell in their followers path. This requires no actual deep rational understanding of the Gurus achievements. Instead, all that is required is the total acceptance of a not understood reality. One follows a Guru by accepting a role which is inferior to that of the Guru, who is often referred to as 'Master'.

We too, have attempted to find a teacher who had all the answers and perhaps even a Spiritual Community who shared our Spiritual goals and upheld the same integrity that we have to reach these goals. We certainly can relate to the desire of many Spiritual Seekers to remain in a zone of relative comfort in which the process of evolution is achieved by following a path already entirely figured out by someone else. We have not succeeded in finding anything remotely similar to what we are looking for and believe to be what is needed for the next step of evolution for the human race. All the Spiritual teachers and Spiritual Seekers that we have encountered have been a blessing and have helped us to better understand that Spiritual Evolution is a process which requires absolute integrity: in intentions, in goals, and in the path chosen to reach these goals. We have learned that Spiritual Evolution requires accepting that evolution is an ongoing process, and will keep being an ongoing process. Therefore, the idea that someone has figured everything out undermines the concept of evolution itself. We have also understood that the ends do not necessarily justify the means. Reaching a goal is as important as the purity of the path required to get there.

Our advice is to look for other Spiritual Seekers to co-create with, who share the knowledge and the understanding of the evolution process being an ongoing evolving process and that, rather than followers, are looking for other co-creators to expand and if needed change what they have already figured out and elaborated. There is a lot of wonderful information that comes from most of the Spiritual teachers and an important part of our contribution is thanks to this information. The steps that follow are to elaborate, filter, and discern all of this information.

We welcome the process of intuitive learning and enthusiastically acknowledge its greater capacity to guide us where our rational mind cannot take us because of a lack of information. Our intuitive side is connected to all of the consciousness in existence, and our rational mind elaborates the available information. As the evolution of the whole consciousness proceeds, the information changes. The gift of intuition allows one to venture into places where our rational mind could not take us. Spiritual Seekers around the world, for a long time, have understood the importance of intuition and relied on it to take them into unexplored territories. Many, however, have not been able to transform their understanding into words that could be understood, and therefore elaborated upon by other Beings. Understanding has been especially challenging for those Beings who lack a developed connection to their higher intuitive capacity but who are gifted with a high objective capacity of structuring their understandings into clear concepts. Often Spiritual teachers have contradicted themselves over and over again. They explained their continuos contradictions was their attempt to open and expand the minds of their disciples or followers. This metaphoric gym to stretch the mind can certainly be beneficial. The main reason for opening the mind, however, is for the mind to be able to learn more and to elaborate more. In order for a mind to elaborate more it requires information which is not continuously contradicting as both evolution and devolution may represent change, but change is not the sole (or soul, in this case!) objective of a Spiritual Seeker. Intentional constructive change is what a Spiritual Seeker seeks— to construct over what has already been built by others before them, and to create something even more sublime.

The most effective way to be co-creators of the Spiritual Evolution of Human Beings is to develop both capacities, intuition and objective reasoning, and connect with others who have also been trying to balance these two complementary aspects. Thanks to rational thinking, humans have been blessed with the capacity to use words. Words have always been used by Spiritual Gurus in their teachings, yet it has been repeated numerous times that what they have reached cannot be put into words. This leaves little room for the Gurus' followers to reach what they are searching for. Concepts are expressed in words and as our concepts evolve, humans have the opportunity to continuously create new words in order to continuously better elaborate these concepts. Rather than sacrificing the capacity to elaborate in words the concepts one has mastered by intuition, we recommend raising the capacity to elaborate with words in order for these concepts to be shared in a way that is accessible to the rational mind and can be shared by all others to allow an ongoing elaboration. The elaboration of Spiritual concepts, as we are doing here in *The Manual of Spiritual Living*, brings a higher understanding of the concepts to those people working with them. Just as in the process of understanding miracles[19], the first step to achieve a goal is for the objective mind to conceive of a rational way to understand it, and then the possibilities are limitless.

We have met many amazingly evolved souls; this is referring to Human Beings who have a high vibration which can be perceived consciously or unconsciously by all around them. These marvelous Beings, we believe, have chosen to embody themselves in an attempt to help other humans to raise their vibrations too. Many of them have an extremely evolved intuitive capacity, although their capacity to rationalize, and therefore express rational concepts, is limited. This has made these evolved souls partially dysfunctional and has immensely limited their capacity to share their

---

19 See: *The Manual of Spiritual Living, Part 2: The Eve of Transformation*...Miracles

evolution with the world in a constructive way. These marvelous Beings have often become frustrated by the incapacity of the world to understand them, recognize them, and celebrate their coming. They have often refrained from developing their rational, objective mind and have not gained a true capacity to elaborate and express their higher understandings. Once more, the unbalance between the masculine and the feminine is responsible for a significant contribution to humans' lack of understanding Spirituality.

We don't have all the answers. We don't believe that any other human that we have encountered on our journey has all the answers either. We are committed, however, to finding them. We believe the answers will change and evolve just as all things continuously change and evolve. What we have been focused upon is the formula which allows impeccable Beings to continuously find and revise the evolving answers. The formula which we describe in different ways and examine in all its aspects is based on continuously being on the lookout for all reliable information and impeccability of intentions while analyzing the new input, adding to the information that was available before, and the information that is available now and balancing the most important tools which we have, which are intuition and objective reasoning.

10

WHAT DO I DO WITH MY EGO?

Many people have heard the phrase, "Let go of the ego" being repeated over and over again. For some, its meaning was immediately crystal clear, while for others absolutely meaningless. Thanks to the wonderful work done by some Spiritual teachers, many have been better able to grasp this concept.

The first step is to identify what the ego is in relationship to who we are. The ego is a personification of who we think we are. Who we think we are, however, is usually limited to a vision of ourselves as the Physical Being acting out a character that we have identified with. The constructed profile is deep and typically buried under several layers of adopted identifications. Many philosophers and thinkers, committed to the research of the true essence of humans, have mistaken the ego for the true self. A well known example, brought to light by Eckart Tolle, is the philosopher Rene Descartes, who coined a famous phrase: "I think, therefore I am." While it is easy for one to mistakenly identify themselves as merely being the ones thinking, many meditators have been able to observe themselves thinking as if they were not participants in the thinking process itself, but actually the Beings observing it. This has also been our personal experience; and therefore, we believe that this means that humans are more than just the ones thinking, and beyond the thinking profile resides our soul.

C.S. Lewis wrote a beautiful and meaningful phrase that helps to better comprehend who one is in relationship to the body and the soul:

> **"You don't have a soul,**
> **you are a soul,**
> **you have a body."**

The implication of this phrase is that the body is an instrument that I, the soul, use on a physical journey. Our interpretation of the relationship between the Soul and the Body, expanded by deductive realization, is that the brain is not likely to be the only "mind" that humans can access. We also believe that the soul is more complex than a mere spark which ignites the body into functioning or animates it into becoming alive. The soul comes into the physical body with a consciousness of its own, which some refer to as the mind, and utilizes the brain for processing information but is still capable of accessing a higher information which we refer to as the "part that knows"[20]. The ego is

---

20 See Ch. 19, Intending..... The part that knows, pg. 142

a creation of our brain which creates an identity for ourselves in a more simplified linear way of thinking.

The mainstream teachings of letting go of the ego have not been clear about explaining the difference between keeping awake our instincts, allowing ourselves to have a rational mental image of who we are, and maintaining an identity which makes us capable of having a functional role in society, while at the same time allowing ourselves to focus on not being limited in our understanding of who we are as the mental image of ourselves as a physical Being. The processes that we have explained in previous chapters such as: **Shedding the Layers, Profiles,** and in Part 2: **Solutions,** and **Opinions**[21], are detailed in explaining how not to be overruled by our brains simple version of who we are, but to honor and respect the ego for what it is.

The ego is the brain's mental image of who we are. It is our belief, as we have mentioned, that the mind is part of our higher self, regardless of the physical body, and is capable of a much more expansive and continuously expanding image of the self. It is not limited by the boundaries of the information gathered while living this physical experience, and it has access to a wider form of intuitively understanding everything. The mind does not require us to have a simplistic linear view of ourselves as the ego does, which uses only the information acquired during the current physical lifetime.

---

21 *The Manual of Spiritual Living, Part 2: The Eve of Transformation*

Once the ego has created an identity for itself it expands its identity by extending it to include personal possessions. The moment in which an object, a phrase, an elaborated thought, a song, or anything else that can be physical or not becomes MINE everything changes. The ego has now claimed it as its own. This also includes a social standing, or a role within the society, a small group of friends or a family. The ego-related value of this something increases the moment in which it becomes a possession. A rock on the road has no ego-related value, but the moment in which one picks it up and makes it "their" rock it immediately becomes something for the ego to protect.

Most humans today are probably not ready to renounce personal property all together. Whether that be physical or mental property, their identities are too intertwined with these objects to let them go[22]. Owning a beautiful house and using it as a sacred dwelling place is different than being attached to the house because you think it is yours. We believe that humans can evolve their perspective about property. Think of your house as a place where, in this moment in time, the Universe has offered to you a place of shelter. Be thankful for it, love it, yet keep in mind that you are not here to collect things, but rather to enjoy what you can with integrity. In other words, we honor personal property but not letting it define who we choose to be.

---

22 We are not advocating a "communist kind of belief", which has nothing to do with evolving the ego, but rather focuses on all egos having an equal amount of property.

Another simplistic and limiting way that people often allow the ego to define them by is the work that they do. *"I am a doctor. I am a realtor. I am a student."* These statements are essentially all false because the truth is that each human is a Divine soul with limitless potential. There are other forms of identification which may be considered more benevolent such as: *"I am a Father. I am a daughter. I am a wife."* It is these identifications that are often used as excuses for less than impeccable behaviors. The role-playing connected to these roles has been entwined with a guilt-ridden form of sacrifice which has been a source of abuse: *"I got pregnant with you. I gave you life. I work hard to provide for you."* The implication of the above is that playing that role forced them to sacrifice themselves and therefore, they expect something in return. Whenever an identification becomes intertwined with debts it creates strong layers, and unnecessary drama, that the ego instinctively holds onto, preventing us from evolving.

Each Human Being on the planet has been a son or a daughter at some point in their existence, but there is a difference between what you are and who you are. Who you are is the choice you are making in every moment.

It is up to the individual to decide if, when and what they are willing to let go of as far as possessions. The process of letting go of personal property tunes in perfectly with the process of becoming impeccable with ones intentions. Each time we think about something which is ours lets start to wonder why it is important to us— and whether the importance is to protect our ego's property from becoming the property of somebody else, or because it is part of some belongings, which for the time being, we are actually nourishing with evolved love and evolved intentions for our own benefit and for the direct or consequential benefit for others.

We are not suggesting here what to keep nor what to give. We are suggesting conscious dis-attachments from all material goods, and letting go of all that you are holding onto for the sake of protecting a mental construct of yourself. Some objects may be better to keep as personal property, but without identifying ourselves with them. A simple example is a toothbrush, and whether or not we wish to share communal toothbrushes with others. We may feel like having our own tooth-brush and that is not because we are protecting our ego from being done wrong to, but because the connection we feel towards other humans and their better or worse sense of hygiene or energetic exchange is not something that we are ready to explore at this stage of our physical evolution.

Each and every day many humans leave behind this world and all that they thought was THEIRS. The truth is that the soul is who they are, and what this world has to offer are tools and toys to help with discovering and becoming their true selves.

11

TO JUDGE, OR NOT TO JUDGE

The main reason for which we are able to write this book is thanks to our ability to judge constructively and thanks to the ability of many other Beings who have judged constructively before us.

Few people have not been exposed to the insinuation that somehow forming a judgement is wrong. Without judgement, however, nothing can improve. How can one improve themselves or the community without first passing a judgement regarding the current state? We feel that the issue of judgement pertains to the impeccability within the motives behind the judgement. So, rather than avoiding judging altogether, use impeccable intentionality in judging the reasons for the judgement itself.

Judgement is a duty, a gift, and a human responsibility. It is our duty, as Beings capable of processing information, to judge constructively as an intentional act of kindness. The question is not whether or not we should judge, but whether or not we have the courage to be intentional in making our capacity of judging a tool with which we can give our contribution to improve all of the scenarios around us.

New-Age Spirituality, in line with many Eastern philosophies, share and have spread a notion for which judgement is considered wrong. Rather than focusing on the reasons and motives for the judgement itself, they both simply created a doctrine for which the enlightened way, the peaceful way, or the right way, of dealing with everything is to practice non-judgement. Other sources regarding the correct interpretation of the teachings of Buddha contradict this theory. Rather than teaching the abstinence of judgement, they sustain that Buddha taught the importance of remaining emotionally untied to the judgement. This does not mean to not feel emotions, but acknowledging the emotions as the lotus flower acknowledges the water all around itself even though it is able to stay afloat, dry and beautiful on the surface.

Some devotees of New-Age Spirituality and Eastern Philosophies would consider our use of the word "wrong" out of line. This is because of another shared doctrine for which there is no right or wrong— a matter for which we have elaborated upon in the chapter Right is Right[23]. We respect their concepts and appreciate that they are in line with the view of Spirituality which relies strongly on intuition. Intuition is part of our feminine capacity to feel concepts. At the same time, we also honor our masculine capacities and

---

23 See: Ch. 12, Right is Right, pg. 104

we cultivate also our capacity to use our rational mind to express intuitive concepts.

Some further ways to describe the New-Age and Eastern Philosophers' feelings towards the act of judgement are:

1. They do not consider the act of judgement as an act which leads toward Enlightenment and/or Spiritual Evolution. 2. Getting rid of judgement is a necessary task for the act of getting rid of the Ego, which they believe to be a necessary step towards Enlightenment. 3. Letting go of judgement means avoiding distractions; and, as a consequence, one can focus on the important task of finding the inner self.

We have set the best of intentions in formulating a judgement over the beneficial aspects of practicing non-judgement for the purpose of Evolving Spiritually. As a result, we have come to the conclusion that the act of non-judgement is often a form of escapism and beneficial only as a practice so that one can discern their motives of judgement and practice self control of the mind. The act of constructive judgement is a form of connecting with and constructively improving ourself and others; thereby, refraining to constructively judge ourselves and others creates isolation and stagnation. We believe that when constructive judgement is in the mix, there is a more fertile ground for creation. Consciously shared judgement creates a communal ground where one can find more seeds for evolution. Consciousness grows as there are more Conscious Beings who plant their seeds and communicate with one another, including constructively and lovingly judging one another, and constructively and lovingly accepting judgement.

We have also witnessed the results of non-judgement from a practical perspective. Many times, the consequence of indulging in the act of refusing to judge inhibits evolution, productivity, financial security, and contributions to the society. Many people attempting to follow the philosophy of non-judgement find themselves focusing so much of their energy in avoiding to create judgement, that they end up missing many of the lessons that the Universe has offered them. We have also observed that they often miss out on finding constructive paths to express their capacities in a more functional and economically rewarding way.

We have expressed how the teachings regarding living without judgement are more mainstream within the teachings from Eastern Religions/Philosophies and New-Age Spirituality. We also want to point out that all of the Polytheistic religions have been responsible for rooting, within a huge number of humans, the concept of surrendering to a more powerful force. The only judge, in their view, is an omnipotent God. God's intervention has been blamed or praised as an all-powerful will not to be questioned. The act of submitting to God's will, which those who follow this doctrine, consider to be the force responsible for all events, has been referenced as a basic teaching one must accept. This has mystified human's capacity to formulate constructive judgements and downplayed our responsibility to do so.

Be impeccable when using judgement.

Judging is often misused as a form of petty self indulgence with which people compete with others by judging others negatively. Judgement, in its lower form, is similar to competition, in its lower form. This is because people sometimes lack impeccable intentions when participating in both judgement and competition. When people compete in the higher form, they do so to better themselves and to better others. When they compete in the lower form, they do so to show how much better than others they are and to gain envious admiration. Spiritual Evolution requires the embodiment of the Higher Self, and hence practicing the highest forms of all behaviors.

Competing has been a useful way for humans to compare their talents. An easy way to find out how one performs compared to others is by comparison. The positive and constructive results that derive from healthy competition are a main factor in what has fueled human achievement. There are negative aspects, however, that emerge when the motives behind the competition are coming from the lower self. The negative consequences of petty competition have been responsible for the expression of many unpleasant sides of human nature. Many people who indulge in the lower form of winning competitions find it utterly important for everyone else not to be as good as they are. Similarly, those who indulge in the lower form of losing, rather than feeling joy in being surrounded by others to follow as an example and feel happiness in being surrounded by people better than themselves, feel pity for themselves.

In conclusion, the action of competing can be positive, as it can can be responsible for improvement; however, it can also be negative, as the motivation behind it can inflate petty comparison, ego, or self pity. This principal goes along with the act of judging. The goal is to always focus on the intentions behind the process of judgement, rather that the act itself. This leaves the individual responsible for behaving with impeccability.

Humans have, and will continue, to go through stages of evolution. During these stages many shifts between extremes take place. Currently we find ourselves shifting from the extreme un-compassionate judgement, to a new extreme form of apathetic non-judgement. These shifts seem to constantly mirror the unbalanced duality prevalent in modern-day society. A more masculine approach, in which an attitude of compassion represents an unnecessary obstacle in an attempt to achieve a result, has shifted to a more feminine extreme, in which common sense must yield to compassion at any cost. We consider it necessary for the Spiritual Seeker to find the path leading them to a balance between the Feminine and the Masculine, where truth and solutions are found. This means common sense and compassion can be held in equal light with a mind set on benefiting all involved for the highest good.

ᛅ

*Judgement is a requisite for forming an opinion;
and, when expressed clearly and properly
articulated, the opinion becomes our contribution to
the process of finding a solution.*

ᛤ

A balanced approach to finding solutions requires the acceptance of the potential consequences involved in the short term, while prioritizing the focus on the rationally predictable more likely outcome. This brings the masculine and the feminine aspects of the human mind into balance with one another. This harmony begins with understanding the distinct characteristics that they each hold. Sacrifice and casualties are often too easily accepted by the masculine part, and often totally unaccepted by the feminine counterpart.

Balancing the masculine and feminine aspects means prioritizing the foreseeable, best possible result. This can be done successfully without trying to force an even 50/50 ratio of masculine and feminine. We are not competing, we are co-operating. The correct balance, depending on the person and the situation, may not always come out as a 50/50 ratio. The goal of the Spiritual Seeker, depending on the issue, the situation, and the understanding of both male and female aspects, is to figure out solutions which create the best results.

All of human endeavors are Spiritual endeavors because we are Spiritual Beings. An attempt to compassionately keep the amount of discomfort, in all of its forms, as low as possible is always favored. Living in truth, however, also requires one to accept that attempting to avoid any short-term discomfort at all costs is not an act of real compassion when the consequences in the long-term will be more destructive and create much more discomfort.

Human Beings are currently experiencing a time period in which they dedicate most of their time to practical problems and practical solutions to their problems. Problem solving is usually a process which falls in the category of rational, linear thinking. This requires a more masculine approach. While this kind of mindset is a good tool for accumulating wealth and comfort, we recognize that when a masculine attitude becomes over-whelming, one tends to loose their focus and ends up dedicating all of their time to material matters. On the other hand, the feminine aspect is the most powerful and amazing tool which we all can cultivate, that helps us to feel, experience, and guide us along the path of Spiritual Evolution— and we believe that Spiritual Evolution is the main reason why we are all here incarnated in a human body.

Our belief is that Spiritual Evolution does not require, nor benefits, from letting go of wealth[24] and comforts. At the same time, letting go of the attachment to them is important, and not living them as an obsession is fundamental. We simply appreciate wealth and comfort. We wish and hope that all Beings

---

24 The term "wealth" is very subjective, and can have very different meanings for different people. Our humble meaning of the word is having a place to live, clothing, and food.

can experience it— which is why we are teaching how to make this possible for others. Our conclusion is that wealth and comfort have the potential to make it easier to focus on Consciously Evolving Spiritually. We are also aware, however, that the continuous seek for wealth and comfort often turns into an addictive pattern. Unless one is able to recognize this pattern within themselves or unless the Universe lends a hand in forcing one out of this addictive cycle, it ends up becoming the sole (not soul) purpose of existing. Unfortunately, this is where many people end up dedicating the vast majority of their time and energy. We have met many people who have had very little in terms of material wealth, and we have met people who have had a huge abundance of material wealth, and all of them were stuck in the same drama for which because of their lack of wealth, or abundance of wealth, they could not dedicate themselves to anything but gaining some or accumulating more.

One of the most important teachings which we keep repeating throughout *The Manual of Spiritual Living*, and which underlines the meaning itself of Being Spiritual, is Being Intentional. The events that come into our life have an impact, and it is up to the individual to make this impact constructive or destructive. Some people are capable of dealing with huge dramas and maintain an attitude of no-drama. Others live all life events as if they were dramas. Everything that happens to us, in reality, is an opportunity for us to intentionally make the most of it and for us to intentionally be the protagonists of our life. Refining the ability to judge everything intentionally is one of the most important acts that an Intentional Being can focus on.

When life events happen to a Spiritual Seeker, they do not just let them pass by without judgement. What does this mean for my life journey? What lesson is there for me with this? What is the Universe telling me? These are they kinds of questions that one will meditate on, and these are very important judgements to make. The concept of bettering oneself and not passing any judgements are in total contrast with one another.

The exchange of expressed intentional balanced judgement, based on verified information between other Beings doing the same thing, allows advancements to take place. There are two ways of verifying the available information, and they both must be cross-referenced with one another. The first method is the intuitive approach, for which we allow our intuitive self to feel or sense the vibration of the information. The second method is to verify the information with a rational mind and be willing to question everything, including what is considered common knowledge as well as what is considered alternative knowledge. Both types of knowledge are less than impeccable in their reliability.

Ones intuition is always available, and sharpening ones capacity of tuning into intuition is an important task of a Spiritual Seeker. Yet, it is very common for all Human Beings to confuse wishful thinking with true intuition. Therefore, it becomes fundamental to cross-reference what we feel intuitively with other reliable sources of information whenever they are available. The results coming from intentional, rational, objective judgement exchanged by Beings whose intentions are to find the truth, rather than preserving their own convictions, creates the building blocks for paving the road to ongoing stages of Methodical Constructive Evolution. This exchange then becomes the foundation on which an evolving belief system based on unbiased, heartfelt, objective reasoning comes into existence.

The process of Evolving Spiritually has similarities with the process of building, as both require a good strong foundation on which to build. When it comes to Spiritual Evolution, new concepts and understandings will manifest, and new higher floors that are safer and stronger will be created when it comes to physically building. Both examples are an ongoing process of improvement and they both benefit, and even require, to be completely inspectable. The easier it is to repair, improve, substitute, and change each and every single part of a building or a Spiritual concept, and the more practical it is and the more likely it is that it will continue to be considered innovative, contemporary, and functional. The quality of a building depends on the quality of materials or information, the capacity to effectively use the material or information, and the integrity in the quality of the assembly. This works in the same manner with the development of a Progressive[25] Spiritual Concept.

---

25 Not intended in the political sense.

Forming intentions is a much more complex job compared to wishing for a building to come into existence and wishing it to look the way one would like it to look. True manifestation[26] requires knowledge of the facts, acceptance of them, and a rational capacity to realize ones concepts into reality. Setting high goals is beautiful and reflects a positive attitude, but envisioning a huge building is not enough for the building to come into existence. Having high Spiritual Visions is also beautiful; however, visions alone are not enough to create a reliable and realistic Spiritual Concept with serious potential for growth. A Spiritual Concept and a building are both birthed from a creative mind and supported by the current available information and technologies.

Again we have covered another example where a rational mind working in unison with an intuitive, creative approach are key components to successfully Living and Evolving Spiritually. The building blocks for the process of Intentional Conscious Evolution are the beliefs created by a process of intuitive and objective judgement. Wishful thinking is replaced by a more impeccable found truth. Spirituality no longer requires a mystical, incomprehensible, and up to interpretation based on convictions lacking evidence approach; but instead, we are approaching it with a balanced formula where we honor our intuitive self in showing us the way, while impeccably verifying all the available information to determine the integrity of the way.

---

26 See: Ch. 21 Manifestation, pg. 154

We construct and pave the road we walk on without taking any unnecessary jumps or leaps of faith. The goal is to remain objective in both the process of finding the truth and creating our reality with a focus on the results that we want to achieve and the true potential we have to achieve it. At the same time, it is important to maintain the awareness that the more elaborate is the construction we work on, the better planning and verification of the available tools are needed. Most importantly, ones reasons for building it must be impeccable. What we choose to build does not need to be a reflection of ourself or an attempt to impose the vision of ourselves to others, but rather a creation that makes this world a better place.

The Manual of Spiritual Living is the result of our best judgements and our best attempt to evolve the concepts that we have learned and express them in a rational way. Learning is a process of discerning what works from what does not work. **That is judgement.** Judging should not be confused with the ego-led confrontational competition with other egos to reinforce their own identity. **Judging with integrity** is the most important tool that we believe humans posses to choose which direction will lead them to become who and what they will become. **Decision is the consequence judgement.** Every decision we make is the result of a judgement and an intention. When deciding which way to go we will utilize our capacity of judging which way is best depending on what our intentions are. **We are all, therefore, the consequence of our judgements.**

We feel that the teachings that come from the New-Age Spiritualism and the Eastern Philosophers regarding the act of judging would be of better service if they would focus more on the intentions rather than the act of judging itself.

Our answer to the question, "who are you to judge?" is:

We are intentional beings who have taken it upon ourselves to be co-creators in an ongoing improvement of humans, the Earth, and all other Beings by utilizing our capacity to judge with integrity and impeccably holding our best intentions.

Humans' capacity for rational thinking makes them Intentional Beings. Intentional Beings form an opinion based on their judgements. Because of the widespread concept which condemns judgement and, in an unclear way, asks people to refrain from using it, many have either conveniently or unintentionally secluded themselves in a place of 'selective judgement'. This has been an escape for those whose commitment to truth is limited to their comfort zone, and has been a trap for those who could not figure out how to impeccably question everything and be free to form a judgement.

Throughout history humans have often found ways to refrain from approaching sensitive subjects as if by not talking about them and pretending that they do not exist they would somehow cease to exist. Non-judgement is another way to avoid honoring our seek for all truths. Rather than not judging, we suggest that Spiritual Seekers are better off refraining from indulging in unnecessary negative thoughts about others, including gossip of any kind, which is not constructive. The mind does not need to be filled with thoughts such as constant chatter about those around them with the sole purpose of making one look or feel better.

Impeccable judgement is the result of a person behaving impeccably in the attempt to form a judgement using a process which utilizes all constructive tools that are available to a Human Being in order to form it. These tools are intuition and objective reasoning, together with the commitment to scrutinize all of the available information. This process becomes impeccable because of the integrity behind the motives of the person forming the judgement, and their un-compromised attempt to avoid being restricted by any boundaries such as domestication and the ego's attempt to hold onto a judgement, not because of its validity, but because of its "ownership". An impeccable judgement is not always right nor perfect, as perfectionism is a process of constantly striving for perfection. Perfection[27] is an evolving concept interconnected with the available and possibly changing information.

---

27 See: Ch. 13, Perfection, pg. 108

12

RIGHT is RIGHT

The commitment to rightfulness is the reason for which a Spiritual Seeker sacrifices the comfort of holding onto an unchangeable idea of what is right. The concept of an evolving right, however, is different from the idea that there is no right or no wrong. It is because of an impeccable dedication to do what is right that this flexibility is warranted.

Many people have misinterpreted the idea of a flexible rightfulness in order to fit a New-Age mold of non-judgement. This is where concepts such as "there is no right or wrong" have been spread. This inevitably leads to a lack of taking responsibility for ones actions, and prohibits improvements from taking place. Evolving Spiritually means bettering ourselves; the path to bettering ourselves entails the necessity to make choices based on the information one has and ones capacity to process this information with clear intentions and an open heart. Constantly choosing what we believe is right will determine who we are. The criteria and the integrity applied each time we make a decision reflects the Spiritual Evolution that we have achieved.

The concept of "there is no right" is merely the other extreme from an "un-questionable right". Both aspects remove the decision making and the judgement from the individual and impose the acceptance of one dogma or the other. Neither concept requires one to adopt a protagonistic approach. Only as the protagonists of ourselves and of our reality, however, can we make decisions with a truly open heart and rational mind.

The consequence of being wrong requires us to be absolutely impeccable in the process of making choices. Many people avoid taking the risk of judgement altogether because of their fear of being wrong. Rest assured, on a Spiritual Path, being wrong is part of the human process and can be embraced as a learning experience. Rather than avoiding to pass judgement as to what we consider to be right, shift the focus on the criteria for which the judgement is made. It is important to analyze whether or not one is acting out of fear; and, whenever one becomes aware of acting out of irrational fear (not actual danger) re-evaluate ones actions to try and face the fear courageously and act out of love.

ي

Allowing oneself the possibility to be wrong is an important requisite to be right.

ي

Each of us is our own guide and we all are following our own path; along the way we might feel like stopping and relaxing before going any further or changing directions. We are all individuals, and as such, we have our own pace, yet this needs not be an excuse to allow inconvenient truths to be disregarded. We are responsible for the consequences of all the choices we make and that includes the consequences of the choices we avoid making.

13

PERFECTION

The Spiritual Path is a path of perfection, not to perfection because perfection is not a final destination. Not that one should seize trying to achieve perfection, on the contrary, it is the journey towards perfection that brings us closer to Higher Knowledge and truth.

Perfection, similarly to truth, is going to be constantly evolving. Many people think that perfection does not exist if it is changing, but that is just an evolving perfection. What is perfect today may not be perfect tomorrow. The fact that it is evolving and therefore changing, does not mean that it does not exist. A pair of bell-bottom pants would have been perfect to wear in the 1970's, but not perfect to wear in the 1980's, for example.

Two very common statements regarding perfection are: "You are perfect just the way you are", and "Nobody is perfect". These statements contradict each other, and yet they both praise the limits too often imposed on the human race. Both statements are used with the same implication of mediocrity, although they are contradictory. When people tell each other that they are perfect just the way they are, they are usually comforting each other by creating a story not necessarily based on an impeccable judgement. What they usually imply is for the recipients to accept themselves as they are. Reassuring others can be honorable, but it can also be detrimental. When these statements come to be posted on a public avenue they become extremely generic. They may even prevent the recipient of this message from wanting to improve themselves. In other words, since it lacks the integrity that only truth carries, then it risks to portray a message for which humans should accept and honor their limitations.

The other phrase, "nobody's perfect", has the same generic and approximative meaning which ends up mimicking the same message as the phrase before. The surface meaning is that we, as humans, should accept ourselves as imperfect Beings and this acceptance denotes humbleness. As evolving Beings, however, we do not need to accept imperfection as a sort of limit which justifies our lack of motivations to go past all limitations. The priority in becoming an Intentional Spiritual Seeker is not to feel good about ourselves. Our priority is to honor the impeccability in overseeing the reasons for which we feel good about ourselves.

Differently than stated by some Spiritual teachers, we do not believe anyone in human form is perfect the way they are. In fact, we are evolving beings and perfection is a path to follow with acceptance of the fact that we are not yet perfect but we are working towards lovingly perfecting ourselves. The teachings that imply that we are all already perfect beings, and therefore do not need to change, often come from self proclaimed gurus who want to defend their self portrait of perfection.

We see perfection as a paradox. There are two scenarios, one is where all is perfect. The eternal moment is perfect, where we can just Be. The other is where nothing is perfect because perfection is beyond what we can truly grasp, as we are imperfect Beings. So rather than focus on perfection, we allow our highest image of Greatness to be our model for perfection. As evolving Beings, we change, and so does the image of Greatness that we strive for.

14

BREAKING HABITS

Pursuing a Spiritual Path means to act according to what we believe to be the highest good. *(Our subjective ideas about what is good may change, but the goal of goodness always remains the priority.)* Inevitably this pursuit will lead to the realization that some of the habits that we have accumulated during our lifetimes will need to be adjusted. Humans, similarly to other animals, tend to be creatures of habit. When these habits are questioned or threatened our internal reaction often becomes one of discomfort met with a feeling of resistance. This resistance may turn into anger; and, this anger should be acknowledged, as acknowledging and understanding it is the best way to realize that it originates outside the highest self. This book will most likely confront you in this way by providing information that if agreed upon, can lead the reader to major life changes. While Heather has had a comfortable transition each time a major life adjustment occurred, Gio has experienced his lower self getting upset many times. What made it easier in the long run was the acknowledgement that this methodical getting upset process meant that the change was likely inevitable and that he looked both funny and ridiculous during those grumpy moments. Our experience has taught us that each seemingly irreplaceable habit that we left behind gave birth to an amazing discovery which was able to fulfill all of the pleasurable side-effects of the habit which was let go.

Whenever the impeccable judgement of an Intentional Spiritual Seeker brings them to the conclusion that something that they are doing is not beneficial to them and/or to others, something has to be changed. There are no other options, excuses, nor comfort zones in which to deny the acknowledgment. When confronted with the fact that some of the habits we are stuck with have a negative influence and effect, we have to evolve into the Beings who let go of those bad habits.

ث

***A better world is the result of individuals
making better choices.***

ث

Another approach to understanding habits is to become aware of which ones have become an addiction. Whenever a habit is so overwhelming that we realize it is enslaving us we may wonder if it is worth keeping. When Gio stopped smoking, many moons ago, there were no health issues involved. What made Gio decide to quit was the realization that his enslavement to cigarettes was bigger than his appreciation for them. This left no other option than to give them up, which he did. It was not even terribly difficult thanks to adopting a vegetarian diet"[28] and pranayama (focused breath) exercises. We will go more in depth about the importance of a vegetarian diet in *The Manual of Spiritual Living, Part 2: The Eve of Transformation.*

One of the most common negative habits of Human Beings is allowing themselves to lie to some degree; and, this is also the very first bad habit to address in order to conquer all of the others. Lying to some degree reflects a common detrimental attitude of Human Beings for which everything is about compromise and approximation. **The intention of this book is to change that attitude and awaken humans to the fact that only by striving for perfection and becoming impeccable humans will they then consistently walk a path towards Intentional Conscious Evolution.** Otherwise, rather than a path of evolution, it is a path where everything goes and evolution is merely something to stumble upon.

We live in a society where most casual conversation relies on much casual lying. For example, it is common in America today for store clerks to ask customers how they are doing. They do not really care

---

28 "Besides agreeing with the aims of vegetarianism for aesthetic and moral reasons, it is my view that a vegetarian manner of living by its purely physical effect on the human temperament would most beneficially influence the lot of mankind."
   - Albert Einstein

to know, nor is the customer necessarily telling the truth when they reply "good", or "fine, thank you". When Gio would visit the States for the first times he would enjoy shopping in the malls and he would often answer the store clerks with a detailed story on how he was actually doing. Then one day he noticed that what the clerk really wanted was for Gio to swipe his credit card and leave. Some clerks may actually care to know, but these kinds of insincere exchanges have become commonplace.

The important thing for a Spiritual Seeker is to realize the importance of bringing awareness to all actions. A habit may be an intentional repeated act which can be beneficial and performed with awareness. Washing daily, for example, is something that as long as the water supply allows it, and as long as it does not become a compulsive disorder, can be salutary. Daily washing, especially when done with intentionality, is part of a good regime for a Spiritual Seeker. The focus of a Spiritual Path is to live life intentionally so all of our actions become a proclamation of a higher expression of who we want to be.

15

COMPASSION

Compassion is an attitude. Being compassionate is an intentional act of love towards other Beings. The focus of this commitment is the attitude towards these other Beings. It is easy to confuse the aspect of maintaining the genuine attitude of compassion with an ego-fed feeling of self-righteousness. This process has led many people to confuse themselves with others in the process, and fall victim to a trickery of the ego where the object of the compassion ceases to be other Beings and gets replaced with self and the focus becomes the preservation of the self-image. This occurs when the ego takes over and the struggle becomes the attempt to protect the comfort zone where one feels as though they are better than others, rather than maintaining the humble consideration for all Beings.

The Age of Pisces[29] has been dominated by a patriarchal minded way of thinking and dealing with problems. The more masculine way to deal with problems has often privileged resolution at the expense of compassion. The shortest way to go from point A to point B is indeed a straight line, but the space in between these two points, for other Beings involved, may be a sacred space which should be left undisturbed. Compassion is the act of taking into consideration the consequences for the disturbance created to these other Beings and avoiding to connect these two points with a straight line whenever possible, if a disturbance is created to other Beings.

During the last 2000 years humans have conquered and destroyed each other, the land, and many other Beings in their path. Survival preceded all other commitments and the occasions for compassion were restricted to scattered events. This has slightly changed for the better in the last decades. Currently, a Country faced with the decision of whether or not to invade another Country must consider that it will have to give justification, reason, and motive to the rest of the world. The days of "Veni, Vidi, Vicit" or "I came, I saw, I conquered" are, at least for now, something of the past. Compassion, to some extent, has become a part of the mainstream attitude.

When Love and purity of intentions are driving us, compassion naturally flows through us. Being

---

29 Approximately the last 2000 years. Many believe that the year 2012 has marked the end of the Age of Pisces and beginning of the Age of Aquarius.

compassionate means to consciously make an effort to humbly take into consideration the struggle of other Beings. Real compassion, however, is not a lack of intervention. It is an attitude which takes into consideration all available information and chooses the most compassionate of the solutions which actually solve the problem. Being compassionate does not mean to be short sighted and make decisions based on a deliberately biased selection of information. Such behavior does not focus on the end result, but rather in preserving a place of self-comfort. This way of behaving is an act of egoism and often degenerates into an act of egotistical self-pity masqueraded as bravery. It will prove to lack compassion when some will end up suffering from a lack of right action.

Many humans love drama, and they love to indulge in it. They are willing to place themselves in a place of danger just for the sensation of feeling sorry for themselves. Misdirected compassion is often a form of self-pity. Often humans decide to make choices that are not based on the true supposition of the most likely outcome. They even purposely ignore the likely outcome in order to perpetrate a reality which is not real and promote an outcome which is unrealistic. They do this to feed their desire for drama and in some ways they feel like they are victims of their own choices. Often choices are made without collecting all of the available reliable information, and without the rationalization of the potential risks involved. This creates martyrdom, since exposing themselves to these higher risks is an intentional act of self-sacrifice. Consequently, to this sacrifice they perceive themselves as victims and proceed to indulge in a sense of self-pity. In short, humans often make the wrong choices, driven by an unconscious desire for drama, which leads them to end up dwelling in self-pity.

Responsible Beings, in order to be true to a genuine compassionate attitude, have the burden and responsibility to learn all that they can when they are participants in a decision making process. Purposeful avoidance to be part of the solution is synonymous with being part of the problem. The results of the balance between compassion and rationalization are likely to be the most successful. Rationalizing is a complex process which requires a commitment to truth, a tedious gathering of all available information, and the capacity to formulate original thoughts when needed. Compassion, along with rationality, are two vital requisites in the enlightened decision making process. True compassion embraces rationality as part of its commitment to a successful positive outcome.

Compassion, in its purest form, is an act of love. It represents a conscious and intentional choice to see everything and everyone with a feeling of love and spare them from suffering whenever possible. Objectivity is the necessary tool to decide when that possibility is not in contrast with the subsequent suffering of others. Lack of objectivity is what can cause compassion to become a refuge where to hide and avoid the highest form of compassion— which is to take responsible actions.

Being compassionate is the act of doing what is right as the priority, which is the highest expression of love. A really compassionate Being feels love in their heart and honors it by willingly taking a stand in honoring the process which arises from an impeccable, objective thought process that has taken place for them to determine the most probable path to successfully reduce the amount of suffering and accomplish the best results for all.

When "compassionate" actions or inactions are lacking objective reasoning, they are likely to become a refuge where some may prefer to hide, rather than dealing with the facts. Compassion then becomes an excuse to justify acting upon irrational fears and choosing cowardice in a situation which may lead to some sort of confrontation. This confrontation refers to any situation where an action is required, forcing the person to be exposed to something uncomfortable. An example could be as futile as having a friend who has a bad body odor, and the compassionate act would be to confront the friend in a loving way so that they can have awareness of the fact that they have an unpleasant smell and you have reason to believe they would like to know that they smell.

A new confused model of compassion has arisen in the New-Age Spiritual World where it has become an opposing force to reason, and an egotistical way to forgive self for inaction. In the case sited above, the pseudo-compassionate way would be to say nothing to the friend, and self-assuring oneself that the motives are not wanting to hurt the friend's feelings. The friend is likely to be hurt in the end, however, because they remain unaware that others may find their body odor to be uncomfortable. Bringing awareness to the friend is only an act of love, in this case, as the only intention is to help the friend.

There are other examples in which the friends issues could cause harm to others, and confronting the friend, in order to prevent harm to others, IS the compassionate action. Compassion is not the alternative to confrontation; in fact, authentic compassion is actualized through acting out of courage. Courage is the force required for a real Spiritual Seeker to truly act compassionately, as it demands impeccability in the process of aligning the heart with the mind for the necessary course of action. Those who have redefined the meaning of compassion as being the alternative to reason call themselves "compassionate" as if the meaning of the word compassion is referred to their love and compassion for others. While instead, the compassion they refer to is focused only toward themselves and their attempt to preserve their comfort zone. This erroneous meaning of the word compassion has mislead many to become "selectively-compassionate" to whatever fits their agenda.

Compassion is the motive to find the courage within to discern the best course of action to benefit others, even at the expense of ones comfort zone.

Compassion has also become a keyword, for some, in the pursuit of personal gain to the point that many politicians around the world often use it to obtain sympathetic supporters. At the same time, they selectively limit the information and take advantage of one of the biggest weaknesses of Human Beings: laziness. The laziness in retrieving the available information mixed with the laziness to use the mind in elaborating this information leads humans to consistently rely on a process of approximation. The "more or less" technique now used in obtaining results is then influenced by the surrounding repetition of fallacy, and consequently all impeccability is lost. This approximation represents one of the key mechanisms that cause humans to lack integrity.

A compassionate attitude means having a commitment to achieve the best results, which means a commitment to increase the possibilities for a positive outcome. When communicating with others, in most cases, maintaining a non-confrontational attitude is preferable. Remaining calm and moderate is actually going to increase the chances of having a successful exchange of information which has more chances to lead to a share of solutions. Even when confronted with reasons for a heated debate, chances of success are higher when one remains with a peaceful, loving, yet confident approach to the issue.

While compassion is an attitude, it is also a force. This is a force that a Spiritual Seeker will utilize. A true commitment to the feeling of compassionate love will allow one to see through the veil of short-term solutions, upheld many times in the name of compassion, although only representing self-preservation of an individual's comfort zone. This force may be the only thing to hold onto in times when the winds of political correctness[30] blow wiping out everything that they find in their path.

The true meaning of compassion has been misused similarly to the misuse of the meaning of peace. Peace is a goal, and compassion is the force and the attitude that helps lead to the goal of peace. Compassion and peace both require a commitment to seek deep inside all of human capacities, as opposed to limiting ourselves to the bare feel-good sensation. Many people have made a name for themselves by preaching peace and using the peace sign as a weapon to fight against those who did not agree with them. This model of behavior tends to disregard the end result in exchange for trying to obtain an immediate compliance to what gives short-term satisfaction to their built up reality.

The simple desire for peace may not be enough to obtain peace. True commitment to peace requires one to view all possible ways to obtain and maintain peace by choosing, with total integrity, the actions that will most likely produce a positive result. Ones commitment to peace, and therefore the commitment to trying to obtain peace, is a choice; but it is also a responsibility. Choosing to ignore what threatens peace

---

30 See: *The Manual of Spiritual Living, Part 2: The Eve of Transformation*..... Political Correctness

is a lack of responsibly towards the self, others, and the principle of peace itself.

Compassion is the force behind the commitment to align the heart and the mind with true integrity to choose the right course of action. The important thing is not to merely prioritize the actions that make one feel good, but the ones that are more likely to produce the best positive results. It is not enough to merely embrace an attitude of compassion, but one becomes it through their actions.

∼

Ones commitment to compassion can be measured by ones right actions.

∽

16

MORALITY

An empowering part of an Intentionally Evolving Spiritual Path is the act of deeply and openly exploring oneself without restraints or inhibitions. The process entails experimentation and enlightened exploration. This will facilitate one to change much and so will change ones moral beliefs. As a matter of fact, if we are capable of really keeping an open mind and an open heart, these moral changes of view might happen repeatedly. This process requires us not to be contained by the walls made by other people's rules. The goal is that ones awakening shall free them from the boundaries imposed onto them, REGARDLESS of what one has been taught to be right or wrong.

This exploration process takes place internally and externally: Internally we will strive to understand and remember who and what we truly were before any of the conditioning took place. Externally, our actions will honor our internal awakenings and we will then elaborate upon them and debate them with others.

While freely exploring ones true self one may find that they would like to express themselves in ways that contradict with the laws of the society. For example, many Spiritual Seekers find themselves wanting to express nudity. It is our natural state, right? Hence, places like Esalen were born, so that those who felt called to outwardly express their nakedness around others could do so without disturbing anyone. One must use common sense while exploring their personal comfort zone of morality and do their best not to impose their personal comfort zone onto others.

The most relevant approach to moral issues is being impeccable with ones intentions. The only restriction which we advise to keep into consideration when figuring out each individual comfort zone of morality is in regards to the potential negative consequence to ourselves, others, and the environment. We recommend restricting the 10 commandments to one:

Impeccably question the intentions and the consequences behind all actions, and always act towards the highest good for all involved.

What is immoral, in our opinion, is the lack of integrity which people often choose when conveniently acknowledging only partial truths rather than making it their priority to find all of the available, reliable information in order to have a larger picture of what the truth is.

When Gio was a child he learned, like other children, that there were many things to be embarrassed about on face level. That included everything which was slightly different from the shared norms of the society. One day, he wanted to walk out of a store because his Father was asking the clerk for a discount; that day Gio's Dad explained to him that a person should only be embarrassed or ashamed for doing something that is wrong. Gio figured out that being different or standing up for what one believes in, although perhaps not shared by others, does not make one shameful. Only wrong actions are shameful, and for this one must be ones own judge.

In the words of William Penn: "Right is right, even if everyone is against it; and wrong is wrong, even if everyone is for it."

Morality, depending on the issues, is typically regulated by rules and laws. The common way that human groups work when it comes to morality is that the minority adjusts or accepts the moral values of the majority. In some cases, even a more aggressive and outspoken minority can force its way into a more submissive majority. The moral values that are chosen by the society, however, do not need to reflect the moral values of an Intentional Spiritual Seeker. The Spiritual Seeker needs to act as an independent thinker and elaborate their own individual moral ideas and try to change the ones that are imposed when in contrast with their impeccable conclusions; however, they also need to protect themselves from persecution.

Throughout human's recorded history there have been countless shifts regarding the moral views on sexual acts. We personally believe that we should honor our sexuality and understand it as best we can. We are seekers of truth, and given that our priority is to never purposely hurt anyone, understanding and exploring human sexuality[31] is an important part of the seek for truth. We believe that the influences of the various mainstream religions regarding morality, including sexuality, are stuck in the time period that they were formulated in and prevent a large number of humans from expanding their understanding of morality and sexuality. We highly encourage each Spiritual Seeker to become an independent thinker and avoid following any of these rules un-questionably.

Humans need to adopt moralities that are not dictated by fear but by self respect. Respect has to be the result of an impeccable judgement over the foundations on which that same respect is built and the reasons for which it is earned.

---

31 See: *The Manual of Spiritual Living, Part 3: Love is Union*... Sexuality

17

RESPECT, NOT SUBMISSION

On the quest of defining and re-defining which moral values one adheres to, a Spiritual Seeker will often be exposed to a command which humans have been repeating to each other over and over again: Respect. Throughout our lives we have all likely been told that we have to respect this or we have to respect that. This implied mandatory instruction, however, is an outright contradiction to the true meaning of respect. Respect is the act of honoring and esteeming something or someone through the process of judgement[32] based on ones reasons for meriting this respect or not. The moment in which the act of respect is contaminated with the implication of a command, the whole definition falls short of any of its original meaning and the real meaning of this command becomes SUBMIT. An Intentional Objective Spiritual Seeker and Unbiased Free Thinker respects that which according to their views, deserves respect. This

---

32 See: Ch. 11, To Judge Or Not To Judge, pg. 88

commonly and widespread command, disguised as respect, but in contrast with its true definition, actually means submission; it is not only erroneously used, but it is a misleading untruth which is not upheld by those who make the demand.

A *Spiritual Seeker* honors other people's free will to make choices but is not required to honor what those choices may be.

When someone tells us that we have to respect something, there are two things to keep into consideration: The first thing to remember is that we do not have to. The second is that they are not respecting us and our free will. Humans have become masters at creating doctrines which trap them into bubbles of domestications and senseless repeated concepts from which they can not get out from. An Intentional Spiritual Seeker respects only that which deserves respect. Just like a warrior chooses his battles, a Spiritual Seeker may accept refraining from confronting all conflicting ideas and differences of opinions. This refraining, however, is not necessarily an act of respect, it is simply an act of selection and prioritization.

Another unfortunate example of how frequently the word respect is misused instead of submit is found within the phrase: "I will teach you respect". It has been repeated countless times prior to or during a beating in which the person doing the beating tells it to the person being punished. Respect ought to be the consequence of merit rather than abuse.

Then we have another subtle and erroneous meaning often given to the word respect which is TOLERATE. When the use of the word respect is not a strict command for submission, then it is often used as a command for TOLERATING. Tolerance is a beautiful concept but it is not another word for respect. Tolerance is the expansion of one's comfort zone which allows different views and consequential behaviors to co-exist harmoniously within one's paradigm. The ambiguity in mixing up the meanings, however, may create ambiguous results. Tolerating something allows for the act of not respecting it, and intentionally allowing it to be without interference. The meaning of tolerance, because of the fact that it is granted without the respect, becomes strictly limited to a form of consent. Consenting to something is a form of acceptance. Accepting something, or tolerating something is an act of kindness. Kindness is an act of love which has to prioritize the recipients. If the kindness prioritizes the abuser above the ones being abused then it is not tolerance but cowardice. There is an enormous difference for an Intentional Spiritual Seeker between respecting something and choosing cowardice disguised as respect, since the Spiritual Seeker is committed to the integrity of all actions and their true meanings.

"Neutrality helps the oppressor, never the victim. Silence encourages the tormentor, never the tormented."~ Ellie Wiesel

18

AWARENESS

Definition of awareness:
knowledge

Synonyms:
aliveness, appreciation, bodhi, comprehension,
consciousness, discernment, enlightenment,
experience, information, keenness, mindfulness,
perception, realization, recognition, sensibility,
sentience, understanding

Antonyms:
ignorance, insensitivity, unconsciousness

Awareness is a state of being. This statement
may sound generic to some, but it is the best way that
we have found to explain the different meanings which
the word awareness takes within the Spiritual world. In
the Spiritual world one of the meanings of awareness is

the conscious acknowledgement of intuitive knowledge. Becoming aware means gaining knowledge while being aware of this gain. This information is intuitively channeled and one is aware of this knowledge being accumulated. Another meaning that has been given to the word awareness is in the phrase **"Being Aware"**. This meaning is also expressed by the phrase, **"Being Present"**. Living while being aware means to be present throughout every act of our daily routine so that each of the many moments become inspiring times of living meditation strengthening our connection between our intuitive self and the Divine.

Gaining awareness is a process by which we increase our intuitive capacity. When we become **aware**, we acknowledge the existence of our intuitive self to a higher degree than previously thought. We no longer "suppose" that we can feel intuitively, we become **aware** of knowing that we can feel intuitively. By acknowledging the existence of our intuitive self, our connection to the intuitive self increases significantly and our awareness becomes a heightened vision into what is not "rationally" known. Consciously empowering our intuitive self enhances our capacity to intuit with greater clarity. A phrase that is often used by Spiritual Seekers to describe the act of being present is: **Be here now.**[33]

---

33 It is also the title of a book written by Ram Dass that is worthy of reading.

*Being present in the moment is a pre-requisite
to intuitive knowledge and it is the first step
towards manifestation.*

To Live Aware is the art of being knowingly present as opposed to living on automatic pilot. The concept of living on automatic pilot is used to describe the process that humans go through during their daily routines without paying any attention to them. They have a tendency to let laziness accompany them throughout much of their life. Every normal day becomes a task of completing a list of "to do's" while trying to reduce the mind's engagement in the task. They tend to breathe without paying any attention to it, consume breakfast as if somebody else was eating it for them, drive to work and spend a whole day doing what in some way they are paid to do, and throughout all of this time they are disconnected from the part of them that knows each single little act of their life could be a Spiritual Awakening.

Many humans have replaced the act of living the day with the the act of *pulling through* the day. In a bigger picture, by doing this, many humans end up *pulling through life* rather than *living it*. Living aware means to step out of the concept of life lived as a grocery list of things one needs to do in the future and replace it with a list with **one** thing, that one thing that you are doing **now**. Awareness is not a one-step achievement; it is an ongoing path of Awakening Moments.

Some years ago we found a simulated computer game that portrays a typical human's life for which the purpose of the game is to satisfy basic bodily functions, to have an ongoing and growing source of income, to increase the size and quality of material possessions, and experience basic social interactions. After playing this game for a short period of time, we discovered a "cheat code" for which we could have unlimited money, and therefore skip right to the part where we could buy all the most expensive virtual luxuries that the game allowed. We instantly found ourselves virtually owning everything that we could buy in the game and eventually lost interest in the process of accumulation and consequently lost interest in the game itself. The important realization that arose was of how vividly this process of accumulation mimics the behavior of people in real life and how this process which is meant to be a part-time activity tends to become the main activity in ones life. This experience helped us to realize that if we were to look back upon a life spent with the main focus as accumulation, we would not have achieved as much as what can be achieved by focusing on making Intentional Spiritual Evolution our main purpose.

Making Intentional Spiritual Evolution a main priority also entails living life as 'Tuned In' as possible. Many achieve 'Tuning Out' by focusing on a distraction, and today's modern society offers countess ways for people to achieve this. The distractions and the materialistic objectives are currently so many that the time dedicated to seeking enlightenment in all of its forms (such as constructive and enlightened conversations which allow an exchange of energy, conscious opinions, intentional yoga, meditation, enlightened sexual exchange, conscious loving, communing with nature, cloud gazing, sun gazing, etc.) has been reduced to a fraction or eliminated altogether and replaced with a constant search for material gains.

We strive to be impeccable when expressing all the teachings in this book; therefore, we will also mention another phenomena that we have witnessed and that is becoming an important factor in modern-day times. During the last 30 years or so, a relatively small, yet increasing amount of humans were born with a Higher Awareness and with a distinctive detachment to material accumulations. These Beings have been given many names, and many believe that the reason for which they incarnated and are incarnating in this time period is to actually raise the awareness of the entire human race. However, most of these individuals found no balance within themselves, nor within the teachings available to them, to become functional within the present-day society. As a result, they ended up being both an inspirational light and a dysfunctional burden upon the society.

These Beings' superior awareness of this world as a world of energy and their profound disconnection to this world as a world of objects allows them to perceive a reality wider and more expansive than other Human Beings, but it does not facilitate them to express what they see in a rational way, nor to make their teachings as productive as they can be if and when balanced with the objective and rational part of themselves. Some of the names that many use to refer to these Beings with a different level of Spiritual Evolution include the Indigo Children, the Crystal Children, or the Rainbow Children. These groups are said to be highly empathic, strong-willed, independent, often considered strange by family, and likely to be inclined towards Spirituality.

Many of these Beings feel underestimated, misunderstood, and unable to bridge their higher intuitive understanding with the contemporary reality. Our objective with this book is not limited to explain the intuitive side of awareness, but also to bridge these people and offer them the tools to become more functional and enable them to better express their higher intuitive understandings in a rational manner. For this to happen they will be required to balance within themselves their masculine with their feminine sides[34]. As we have already expressed, this alludes from sexual orientation and gender. This balancing is an intentional act of cultivating both sides of human's remarkable complementary capacities. It is also important to discern within both the masculine and the feminine, those aspects which we refer to as the negative masculine and the negative feminine. Once more, this is an intentional recipe and acknowledging the existence of both negative sides and consciously discarding them is the right thing for an Intentional Spiritual Seeker to do. This is about honoring ONLY the constructive positive masculine and positive feminine.

---

34 See: Ch. 3, Duality, pg. 32

Conscious Spiritual Evolution means evolving Spiritually; gaining awareness and being Aware (present) all of the time are essential parts of the evolution process. By gaining awareness, we acknowledge our connection to our intuitive self. By acknowledging our connection to our intuitive self, we are sharpening and strengthening our connection to the Divine. By becoming aware of our level of evolution, we can methodically work towards consciously evolving ourselves. Being aware at all times helps us to transform every moment into a moment of Spiritual Evolution.

Awareness, similarly to other concepts which we have elaborated upon in this book, is a path which has to be followed with impeccable intentions, and therefore with an impeccable focus. We are the result of our choices. Our choices come from our experiences combined with our intentional adjustment of our actions to make our awareness a continuos growth.

19

INTENDING

༄

Aligning oneself with the goal of reaching a higher awareness is facilitated by a process called intending.

ༀ

Intending is an internal command that we give and carry out by aligning our subconscious self with the objective that we desire to reach. This is accomplished by synchronizing our rational mind with our intuitive self. We have adopted two names that we feel better describe these two:

The part that **Thinks** and the part that **Knows**

The part that thinks is the part of us capable of using deductive reasoning and rational thinking. It draws upon information and reaches conclusions based upon a linear form of thought. The part that knows does not process the information, rather it feels the information directly as a form of intuitive wisdom.

The part that knows is experienced both consciously and unconsciously by all humans in many different ways. Some of the ways have been given a name which defines the phenomenon but humans have yet to give a clear understanding or an objective theory as to the source from which the phenomenon is generated. One example is what is commonly referred to as instincts. It is an established fact that all animals have instincts, and for this the term *"animal instincts"* is used.

The available results of the research done regarding where these instincts are generated and stored is very limited and approximate. There is a commonly accepted theory for which instincts are a form of memory stored within the genetic code (DNA). The study of genetics is indeed able to explain physical appearances and bodily structures, but it has yet to explain how instincts can be stored in the form of "Instinctual Knowledge" in regards to unlearned behaviors. Most animals demonstrate instinctual behaviors which allow them to perpetuate the cycle of life. They breed instinctively, care for their off-spring instinctively, and even co-exist following instinctual behaviors that are not adopted by experience, but only by instinctive gain. For example, birds know how to build a nest, although they have no memories of how their parents did it, and there are an immense variety of different ways to build a nest. Similarly, newly hatched sea turtles will automatically venture towards the ocean, even though they are born on land. Baby kangaroos climb into their mother's pouch upon being born. These are just some examples, as there are a multitude of known imprinted behaviors that we humans, thanks to our objective rational mind have been able to witness, study, and prove consistent within all of the enlarged animal kingdom.

The study of DNA has been successful only in proving physical patterns stored in the genetical coding. The implication for which all the information is stored in the physical form, however, is only theorized. On the other hand, there are more and more studies that are successfully proving that there is a connection to all knowledge and that all creatures can access this "Universal Knowledge". This connection is best described as intuition. Perhaps the DNA coding is part of our physical key to access this knowledge rather than a limited amount of information stored within us that is virtually unchangeable. To better understand this concept one can imagine every creature with a coded key which grants them entrance into the Universal Knowledge but only to the particular part of knowledge that their key unlocks. It is important to keep into consideration that evolution is possible for all creatures and that by evolving we gain access to more of the section that we have initially started with. Many Spiritual Masters claim that they can see the normally invisible lines of energy that connect all things, and they claim that the reason why they can see this is because of their "higher" evolution which allows them to access a larger spectrum of knowledge.

This Universal Knowledge has been described in many ways, including Collective Consciousness, God, Divine, All that is, Unified Universe, We are all One, and more. The part that knows is the part of us which is able to tap into this Universal knowledge.

We believe that Universal Knowledge is the collection of all the conscious experiences; and, the expanding Universe expands because of the new information continuously inputted from the experience of all Beings. The part that thinks is the one that allows humans to function even when they are not able to retain awareness of their connection with this shared source of knowledge. It is, however, much more than a "survival" skill, because it allows us to evaluate ourselves impartially on how we utilize free will by allowing us to make choices without clear knowledge of the outcome. This illusion of not knowing the outcome of our actions brings us to the place in which we are responsible for the motives for all actions.

The part that thinks is the part of us which we identify with most of the time. We use it to process information on a daily basis, asses risks, create strategies to achieve goals and to perform other deductive reasoning procedures. The part that knows is referring to the gut-feeling, heart-feeling, intuition, and other terms given to describe how the body communicates information to us. We all have experienced a heightened sense of clarity, at one time or another, that occurs whenever we successfully tap into the part that knows. During this connection we feel like everything makes sense. It is also during these same moments that we experience the feeling of being able to have immediate access to an "external" source of information not limited to our own personal experiences or learning. In those moments the existence of a Universal Knowledge that links all Conscious Beings becomes an obvious reality rather than an abstract mystical concept.

The reason for setting an **intention** is to obtain a result. When the part that knows and the part that thinks are in balance, intention can be set, and consequently the goal can be reached. The part that knows is able to guide our actions without approximation or guesswork, as it *knows* the path to reach the result that we have intended. Many Spiritual Teachers have spoken about the act of intending, including one of our favorite authors, Carlos Castaneda. He describes it as a process by which an order is given to a part of us, which will execute the order without the possibility of error. Intention, in Carlos' words, is the opposite of trying. It is when every cell of our body believes without a doubt in a certain outcome.

Some Zen practitioners claim they can shoot an arrow in a precise spot without aiming for it or even opening their eyes to look at the target. Their philosophy is that if they can intend that the arrow and the target are one, then there is no other place for the arrow to go except on the target. Sportspeople have many ways of describing this same phenomena, that some refer to as "the zone", and all can agree on a feeling that they perceive when they know in advance that they will accomplish their goal. When Basketball players are in "the zone", they know before the ball leaves their hands if it will enter the basket. Similarly, many times we will know when we throw a piece of crumbled paper into the waste bin whether or not we are going to succeed right before the act of throwing it.

An intention can be set for an immediate result, such as the examples mentioned above or it can be set for something to happen in a recurring way. As an example, some people are able to set an intention in their mind to wake them up at a certain hour every morning, and at will they can change this wake up time, always managing to wake up exactly at the hour they have decided. This is a result from setting an intention.

Gio got his puppy Maltese, Mandy, when she was a tiny little creature in size (although not in personality). The first night that they spent together she decided that either she was going to sleep in the bed next to him, or they would both stay awake. Now Gio's conflict was in how to prevent himself from accidentally hurting her while he would unavoidably move in his sleep. That is when he set an intention. Sometimes out of need, other times out of a simple choices, we are able to decide the outcome and synchronize ourselves to a higher degree, then something just happens deep inside and instantly the outcome is clear. Instantly Gio knew Mandy would not be in danger. The message or order had reached a place where maybes are not options, there are only certainties. The body would add to its spectrum of movements a new information that would apply and limit or control it and would sense the creature in the bed with such an awareness that would completely prevent him from accidentally hurting the puppy. Mandy ended up sleeping safely in the bed, next to Gio and Heather, for many years that followed.

Intending is the process by which you set in motion an intention to the Universe. It is an order that you allow yourself to give to a part of yourself that is normally out of reach from the conscious mind. A successful intention is achieved when the part that thinks and the part that knows act together simultaneously. The part that thinks needs to trust the intention without any fear or doubts; at that time the part that knows can accommodate the clear, concise, open and trusting request from the part that thinks.

The goal of a Spiritual Seeker is to establish an ongoing clear connection with the part that knows. While always honoring the part that thinks, slowly and with much practice one can establish a perpetual connection with the part that knows which actually supersedes the part that thinks. The actions of daily life can connect one to the part that knows so that ones life becomes a chain of ever occurring happenings with a higher meaning and a higher purpose. Doubt, fear, and worry slowly dissipate in the awe and wonder of witnessing how easy life can be when we tap into the amazing human potential within the act of Intending.

20

REMEBERING

We believe that Awareness happens also as a consequence of Remembering memories that do not belong to this physical experience. This is because these memories trigger within us a sort of wake-up call to the notion that we are not only the Beings living this physical experience, but Beings whose consciousness pre-dates our physical birth.

There are moments, while being Awake[35], in which many people feel like they awaken to the knowledge that the physical life is a dream. This feeling is triggered by a similar sensation that one would describe from experiencing a deja vu. For an instant one perceives their whole physical life as if it was a very long and vivid dream. It is in this instant that one experiences a seemingly lucid sensation of knowing that physical existence is all but one layer of consciousness. This sensation is also similar to the one

---

35 See: Ch. 24, Awakening, pg. 180

experienced from being awakened from a deep sleep during which we were having a very involving dream but we were not aware of it having been a dream. When that happens, one feels pleased or saddened by the realization that it was just a dream and can often choose to get back into the dream and forget the realization that it was a dream.

Many Spiritual Seekers have used the word "*remember*" while implying a different meaning to the one commonly used. The alternative meaning that they are attributing to *remember* refers to a memory of something that is not part of one's known life experiences; this meaning is in contrast with the common definition of *remembering* which limits ones memories to the current physical journey.

We endorse the theory that these memories, which are not conscious memories from this physical existence, come from prior knowledge belonging to our Spiritual Self. Our Spiritual Self is connected to the knowledge of the Collective Consciousness. When we Remember, we are actually tapping into our memories from that knowledge. A fundamental concept of Spirituality is the acknowledgment that everything that exists is linked together, and we can tap into that knowledge simply because it is part of us as we are part of it. As conscious Beings, we have been part of All-That-Is in some way since day one, hence the reason for which *remembering* occurs.

All-That-Is can be better described as the Collective Consciousness, which we believe to be able to tap into, as potentially all humans may be able to. Some become aware of it only sporadically, however. Many humans choose to ignore this connection while others enjoy it so deeply that they often forget that as long as they are living a physical experience they would benefit much from it, and it would be of much benefit to others, if they would translate the information gained in a rational manner rather than only feeling and enjoying the connection. When a human intentionally dedicates a part of their life to awareness[36] and becomes aware of this connection, they become aware that their memories about the Collective Consciousness clearly seem to pre-date the date of their birth.

We have expressed and explained in the previous chapter our understanding of the concept of Collective Consciousness. This interpretation is very similar to the one shared by other Spiritual Seekers. The idea is that there is a shared knowledge which unites all of the knowledge from all Human Beings that has been accumulated since the beginning of time. The Collective Consciousness is, at least in part, what many refer to when mentioning phrases such as, "*we are all one*". Accessing this Collective Consciousness has been the process by which many Spiritual Seekers have gained higher understandings. In fact, it is our capacity to access this Collective Consciousness which is partially responsible for the coming into existence of *The Manual of Spiritual Living*. We feel that we have expanded on the concept of tapping into this consciousness by applying a technique of rational objective thinking to all Spiritual matters, including the

---

36 See: Ch. 18, Awareness, Pg. 134

process of communicating the information that we have gained from this Intentional Connection.

Tapping into the Collective Consciousness can be a challenging and intense process. When it becomes a procedure that we are able to accomplish intentionally at will, however, it becomes effortless. Establishing a connection with the Collective Consciousness is only part of what is necessary in order for the information to be beneficial to the Spiritual Awakening of more Beings. The information gained by connecting to the Collective Consciousness has to be elaborated thoroughly in order for it to be constructive. This requires a linear-left-brain-rational-masculine way of operating to complement the unbounded-right-brain-intuitive-feminine-capacity, which is the one responsible for granting us access to the information in the first place. In our vision, the Spiritual Awakening of more Beings will be greatly facilitated by the impeccability in discerning the information and the objectivity used in expressing it. The Impeccable Truth Seeker has to honor their commitment to expand the process of achieving and sharing the information, by using the formula of balancing the intuitive self with the rational self.

21

MANIFESTATION

The meaning of Manifestation in the Spiritual World is referred to the shared belief that humans have the power to create their own chosen reality. In other words: "*Manifest* their own reality." This belief is a direct consequence of the theory for which everything is all connected; since it is because of this connection that we can influence everything. All Beings co-exist in the same expanding Universe and contribute to its continuos expansion through their thoughts. We, therefore, are co-creators of the Consciousness in which the expansion is made of. These are both new and old theories: new in the scientific world, and old in the Spiritual world. Now is the time when Science and Spirituality can unify their theories, just as individual human evolution is achieved by the unification of the left and right brain, so will humanity as a whole evolve when these two aspects unite. An intuitive heart felt approach to knowledge is just as important as having an astute objective approach.

Manifestation is a form of *intending,* as it is a process by which one intentionally influences a situation to create a desired outcome. The main difference between *intending* and *manifestation* is that *intending* is mostly a process by which we directly affect ourselves while other sentient beings are only affected by the ripple effects of our internally focused work. Setting an intention is an order which we give to ourselves and carry out ourselves. The process of manifesting, on the other hand, is an outward process as it overlaps with the *manifestation* of other Beings. This means that ones' will and desire overlaps with the wills' and desires' of others and therefore it is subject to limitations. In other words, when we intend, we are affecting our close reality and we are the ones in charge of carrying it out. When we are Manifesting, on the other hand, we are one of the forces participating in creating the reality we wish for, but there are many others simultaneously attempting to create the reality that they wish for and it may or may not be in tune with our desires. When we give orders to ourselves it is up to us to obey them but when we give orders to a shared reality then these commands are diluted with others' commands which may not be aligned with ours. This added challenge is no reason to avoid manifesting ones desired reality, it is, however, a very good reason to become more constructive and methodical with ones approach.

John Lennon used to spread the slogan, "War is over if you want it". We believe that his intentions in spreading this idea was to attempt to manifest war being over as a reality. The idea was that if enough people synchronize their manifestation then there is likely going to be an effect. John was a pioneer in many aspects of Spirituality and Consciousness and we are very grateful for his contribution. In order to successfully create a platform where Manifestation becomes a dependable tool for achieving results, however, we first have to master the implications and the understanding of it.

Constructive manifestation begins with discerning the difference between what is real and what one wishes to be real. If one is choosing to manifest a better reality, it will not happen by refusing to become aware of the existing reality. The task of influencing reality carries with it immense responsibilities and an unwavering commitment. It takes impeccability and courage to seek out an unbiased truth along with a child-like innocence, free from domestication and conditioning, to see reality for what it is. There is power derived from a clear understanding of the way things are, and truth is the key that unlocks our abilities to influence this unified field of Universal Consciousness. Any refusal to face reality, especially when motivated by preserving our comfort zone, creates a weakness in our will and hinders our abilities of true manifestation. This is the fundamental difference between wishful thinking and true manifestation. This confusion between the two is one of the biggest obstacles keeping humans from actually manifesting their desires. The slogan "war is over if you want it" is reminding us that we indeed have the power to end the war if we choose to, but war does not end simply by us convincing ourselves that it does not exist.

Knowledge is power and truth is the key to access that power.

The greatest weakness of Human Beings is in their tendency towards approximation. Things are what they are, and they may not always reflect the way we want them to be. We can affect them, but in order to do so effectively we first have to find the courage within to see things for what they truly are. What we see currently happening is that most people refuse to view reality because **they believe that viewing what is real and manifesting a reality are the same thing.** Humans who are aware of their power of co-creators are often scared to see the truth for fear of being responsible for that reality. Fortunately that is not the case, since manifestation is the result of Conscious Intention, and having true knowledge of the reality is a requirement for successful manifestation to occur.

Acknowledging a reality and manifesting a reality are two different things. In order to change a reality, we first must understand what the reality actually is. Once we have a clear understanding of the way things are, then we can set an intention to manifest something different. A Spiritual Seeker has an obligation to manifest only for the highest good of all involved. This may sound complex in theory, however setting this as part of the intention is actually quite simple. Whatever one may manifest, whether it be for the healing of another or for a war to end, it is of utmost importance, and we cannot stress this enough, it is fundamental that each manifestation be accompanied with the intention for it to manifest for the highest good of all involved. With these tools, humanity can create miracles. Let's co-create together an Earthly paradise where all Beings are happy and free.

An Impeccable Spiritual Seeker does not avoid to acknowledge reality, instead they learn as much as possible in order to make it better.

Hey Jude, don't make it bad
Take a sad song and make it better
Remember to let her into your heart
Then you can start to make it better

Hey Jude, don't be afraid
You were made to go out and get her
The minute you let her under your skin
Then you begin to make it better[37]

---

37 "Hey Jude" Lyrics, by John Lennon

22

DOMESTICATION

(Who are we?)

Have you ever wondered who you would be if the circumstances of your upbringing where changed? If the lessons that were taught to you as a child were different? What you would be like having grown up in a different part of the world, or with different parents? This Spiritual Soul search brings one to examine what is called *domestication*.

Domestication is a term that some Spiritual Seekers use to describe the process in which humans are trained to fit into a certain culture, religion, household, social status, peer group, tribe, or any other conglomerate of people. There is little difference between the domestication of pets, and that of humans; both are trained for the purpose of education in order to allow them to fit into an organized social order, and in both cases it is achieved through a process of punishment and reward. There is nothing inherently wrong with domestication, as any pet owner or parent can confirm. Without any domestication we would only rely on intuition and everything would have to be learned through experimentation. This could be a more evolved way of learning; however, we believe in a balance between intuition and objective reasoning. This means that until humans are evolved enough to connect directly to their higher selves and access the knowledge from the Collective Consciousness directly, many things will have to be learned in a more traditional manner.

The rules of domestication are mostly derived through a process which groups have learned to pass on knowledge through subsequent generations. Domestication can be used for a wide variety of purposes, many of which can be destructive. People are taught fear, jealousy, hate, lies, pain, and many other forms of suffering in the course of their domestication. This is the mechanism for which most people will repeat to their children whatever was done to them as a child. The human mind, similarly to other animals, is designed to imitate the behavior of the Beings that surround it. As co-creators however, it is in our power to be protagonists in this life which requires us to gain awareness of the process of domestication and its ramifications.

The act of being aware includes realizing that
most of what we believe to be our opinion is, in
reality, the result of one or many of our
domestications.

There are various kinds of domestications: family, cultural, religious, governmental, and peer, to name a few. Family domestication is usually the most prevalent of all. This is because at a very young age the imprinting that we receive remains deep within us. As children, we have little or no rational capacity to discern the lessons and tend to accept information unquestioningly. Most humans learn their basic functions from within the family unit. That includes speech, eating habits, and social skills. This kind of domestication is usually relatively easy to recognize within ourselves, because we can identify the teaching with 'Mom' or 'Dad'. Many times we find ourselves voicing a phrase, and thinking, "that sounded like my Mother/Father speaking". Several times it has happened to us, and it was so clear that we had the sensation of hearing our parents voices within ourselves. Becoming aware of the imprinting, by noticing these episodes, can help to create the necessary dis-attachment useful for one to evaluate whether one wants to keep the lessons as part of who one is or change them because of who one wants to become.

Typically there are several different domestications influencing an individual belief system. For example, Gio was born in Northern Italy, but his family was originally from Southern Italy (Sicily), and as soon as he reached maturity he began to travel and spent much time in the USA. There are 3 different cultures at play forming his domestication, each of them different. Thanks to our human capacity to adapt, the result will be a cultural domestication that somehow embraces and discards parts of each of the three, and at the same time, allows him to fit into all three. Having more than one cultural domestication is a blessing, since it becomes much easier to identify the existence of each domestication because of having three different ones to discern from, rather than living one of them as an absolute truth not to be questioned.

A prevailing technique that has been wisely adopted by the New-Agers to unite people into the peace and love paradigm which they wish to shift to, has been to focus on the similarities between cultures. In our experience, however, gaining awareness of the differences is just as important. In the case of dealing with three different cultures, for example, acknowledging the negative aspects and focusing on eliminating those has been beneficial for Gio in breaking through the restrictive boundaries of his domestications.

A common misconception that humans tend to adopt is to believe that they are free thinking individuals while behaving purely as the result of their domestications. This happens as the result of defending the identity formed around the belief system in which they were born, rather than searching for the identity which defines them because of their intentional choices in becoming the most Evolved Being they can conceive of. The only way in which we can find out whether we are re-enacting what we have been taught to be or whether we are continuously transforming ourselves into who we want to become is by deeply questioning everything about who we think we are.

The negative repercussions of hidden and un-questioned domestications are numerous and they represent a threat to Spiritual Evolution in all of its aspects. Imagine a scenario in which a wide spread group of people methodically teach their children to memorize "the way things are". The way they do this, in order to make sure that these teachings are implemented without hesitation, is with realistic threats of scary consequences. The teachings, in this imaginary scenario, include making sure that the process of imprinting the coming generations is consistent and ongoing. This indoctrination process includes the acceptance of the teachings as absolute truths. This unfortunate scenario is actually quite common amongst humans and it is almost impossible to overcome unless it is brought into awareness. The commitment, for those Beings who believe that Spiritual Evolution requires the absolute freedom to question the teachings and to be able to discard them, is towards recognizing the peril of these absolute dogmas. Once awareness has brought these dogmas into the light, then the commitment is in trying to bring this awareness to those who are not aware of the "spell" that makes them believe that there are absolute truths that require punishing when questioned. This process of indoctrination repeated perpetually and with no room for change represents a very big threat for the whole human race and Intentional Spiritual Beings may consider intervening by interrupting it when they find it on their paths rather than submitting to it under the false pretense of tolerance[38]. Most importantly, however, is not to adopt the lie as the truth in order to find acceptance. An Intentional Spiritual Being considers acceptance an honor only when it is acquired with the maximum integrity on the part of all involved. If that acceptance process is an act of adjusting to layers of lies, then it is in contrast with the integrity that defines impeccability.

Our own experience has taught us that to be totally honest with ourselves is a task requiring the utmost impeccability. *Removing the layers of partial lies, and memorized opinions is a similar process to removing the layers of an onion, as many truths and lies become revealed through tears.* Releasing to our partner the trust of becoming a mirror of ourselves has helped us immensely. It has greatly accelerated this process and prevented us from straying from our path. This can be obtained only by granting the partner absolute trust and the absolute trust can be granted to a partner only after it it has been first granted to ourselves. It has been a long time for us since we first adopted an unconditional path of truth towards ourselves, to each other, and in all dealings with others. The intentional path of impeccability that we have adopted and that we

---

38 See: Ch. 17, Respect, Not Submission, pg. 130

support and recommend for others to follow calls for exposing ourselves and everybody else to the scrutiny of unbiased truth. It has not been chosen by us because it is an easy path, as it is likely to awaken much drama whenever we expose ourselves and others to the realization that we are re-enacting a part that we have been domesticated to act. It is however, the path that is necessary to accomplish Intentional Conscious Evolution.

23

CULTURE

(Cultural background domestication)

One can be proud, not of the cultural traditions that they uphold, but rather in those they have discarded when those domestications do not align with who they choose to be. If we examine the cultures of the last thousands of years, and what shape humanity has been into, we do not get a very pretty picture, and most of the cultural traditions that have survived the decades have been those of oppression, deprivation, abuse, and a blatant disregard for the planet and the other Beings that we share it with. So apart from a very small minority, most cultural traditions that we all come from are best left behind so that a new, improved, human family can emerge.

Once a child begins life outside of the home, and begins interacting with people of the society new kinds of domestications come into play: institutional, cultural, religious, and political. At the present time, most of the world widely accepts being somewhat critical of our political and religious beliefs. On the other hand, it encourages cultural domestication and advocates people to embrace, defend and even create new forms of cultural domestication.

ॐ A Spiritual Awakening ॐ

We have not come into this physical experience to belong to something— a group, a political party, a country, a religion, a race, a culture, an elite, a tribe, or anything else like it. We are here to belong to ourselves, to shed the layers we were brought up with and become intentional about who we want to be. It is not an enlightened act to live a life defending beliefs that we have blindly adopted, as they are not based on our impeccable original thought process and constant acquisition and discernment of information. We are responsible for opening up the minds and the hearts of those groups, that party, that country, that religion, that race, that culture, those elite, and that tribe. How we make a difference is by taking the responsibility to break down those boundaries not only out of impulse, but out of an intentional combination of intuitive and rational processes and an ongoing understanding that evolution is a work in progress and openness to change is the only way to let that process unfold.

ॐ

As we go through childhood, we are like sponges, and tend to absorb the information delivered to us unquestionably. We trust the people we love and that raise us, and we expect them to have it all figured out. In return, these elders expect us to honor them by obediently fitting the profile that they have prepared for us. The influence that hits us is not limited to our close family, but it expands to all the people around us: schools, media, friends, religious institutions, teams, and more. Out of all this information that we are exposed to, we are likely to become a mixture between what others expect us to be, the way they see us, and who we feel we are. We will try to identify with what we feel more represents who we want to be at that moment. These same expectations from others and from ourselves will continue as we grow into adulthood; in particular, we will be expected to uphold and defend our cultural background, stick to the religious beliefs in vogue around us, and choose a political side.

It is quite common for people to adopt their religious belief, political ideas and their cultural background from the environment they grew up with. Changing any of the above is a scary process for humans, as it requires not being anymore part of something they are accustomed to and wondering out of their comfort zone. Today, in most of the Western world, it is considered acceptable to question religion and most are aware of how these different beliefs separate people. It is also accepted that politics may be a cause of separation. These acceptances entitle us to be able to use and express a critical process while we analyze the different beliefs. Instead, cultural background is still lingering in between what is considered politically correct, therefore untouchable, and what is acceptable to question.

A phrase commonly repeated is, "we have to respect other people's culture". We are taught to tolerate something unquestionably, and at the same time denied the right to choose if this is worthy of our respect[39]. Mixed in the potpourri of cultural backgrounds are some virtually harmless forms of art, such as: architecture, dance, food, language, clothing, painting, music, sculpture, etc. We honor all forms of artistic expression when they harm none. Too often, however, concepts such as violence, submission, dominance, abuse, and taboos, linked to the honor and reputation of a 'good' man or 'good' woman are protected under the veil of culture.

Gio grew up absorbing much of his mental image of himself through his Sicilian family and the teachings derived from it. For many years, he was dedicated to fit into this profile which included being a good 'honorable' Sicilian. One small doubt about whether he was actually a 'Sicilian' rather than the Sicilian being a role that we was taught to play was all it took for him to decide to verify if that is what he wanted to be.

Most humans living in an organized society are wrapped in multiple layers of teachings that shape their belief system; most have been proudly wearing these wraps for so long that they are not conscious

---

39 See: Ch. 17, Respect, Not Submission, pg. 130

anymore that it is in fact not part of their being. Many will struggle and become extremely defensive when confronted with the idea that their beliefs are not their own. In most instances, they have likely been adopted without question from a young age. A monumental step towards awareness happens the moment that we realize this. Realizing is merely the first of many steps, however, as the undressing of the layers is an ongoing and challenging process. Being Aware encompasses everything— including the act of being aware of the fact that we have been domesticated. This is regardless if any actions will be taken to preserve it, partially get rid it, or eliminate it entirely.

Sicilian culture has much in common with most of the old cultures of the planet we all live on. It has a very strong male dominating mentality, and prides itself with many similar issues on how a man is supposed to behave and how a woman is supposed to behave. Some words such as honor and pride acquire a new meaning in the cultural context. This meaning becomes so important that it will even justify unmentionable acts of violence.

The moment in which we realize that we are having doubts regarding our agreements and the teachings coming from our culture, we are faced with a choice: Ignoring the doubt, and therefore abandoning oneself from the evolution process. Or, choosing to follow the only path for an Impeccable Spiritual Seeker, which is to **accept the change and seek the truth**. The truth being our highest interpretation of what is right, given the information we have at the time. This will inevitably, at some point, translate into letting go of the culture, as either a culture evolves with us, or it is our duty to evolve alone without the comfort that comes from belonging to a cultural group of Beings. This process takes a continuous effort and a continuous state of alertness.

Once we become accepting of the necessity to move on from our culture and are willing to adventure into the unchartered zone of the self-discovery territories, then it is time to do this methodically, not merely as a onetime adjustment. When the process begins we shed the first layer of the mental construct that we had created in accordance to the teachings of the culture we inherited. This is the just beginning, however. The process takes time and determination to become aware of the numerous layers that we have enrapt ourselves in during our life journey, without ever having realized.

The multitude of similarities between older cultures around the world show a very common link regarding the issue of the treatment reserved to the females of the human species. The feminist revolution that brought light to the United States has likely been a consequence of the mixture of many diverse cultures, and the consequent watering down of indisputable dogmas. This is the reason that has initially alerted us to notice the negative effects that derive from holding onto stagnant beliefs dictated by human's fear of letting go of behavioral patterns and the reason for them to change very slowly. We accepted as reasonable the shared belief of people around the world, including Americans, that "Americans have less culture", and we took it as a positive sign. Yet, we have come to realize that a culture does not necessarily have to be rooted in ancient times in order to be engraved in the consciousness of its citizens.

Heather, having a Canadian-American background, found herself reviewing issues which Americans considered indisputable. She realized that many of the seemingly indisputable arguments were simply a form of cultural domestication and did not uphold to a higher truth. One example happened to us last night while we were venturing into reviewing the unquestionable, indisputable cultural truths around the First Amendment of the Bill of Rights. Ours is a commitment to the seek for truth, regardless of the consequences, so we will not hesitate to question everything. For example, part of the document states that *"Congress shall make no law respecting an establishment of religion, or prohibiting the free exercise thereof"*. Thus granting immunity to all established religions, and potentially creating a State within a State. Humans have the right to believe in whatever they choose; however, religious rights do not surpass the rights of an individual, in our opinion. Religions can be free, as long as the religion itself does not require its followers to break the common laws. We are aware of the current beliefs regarding the implications of the First Amendment, which appear to embrace the concept for fears of legislation prohibiting the practice of one or more religions. We feel, however, that religious immunity is taking that right too far.

The American Forefather's intentions in writing the Bill of Rights was not written for religious laws to surpass the wishes of the majority of the people. This law was added to the Bill of Rights because the forefathers wanted to make sure that the government that they elect could not dictate over the religious beliefs shared by a voting minority. When the Bill of Rights was written they felt their duty was to protect religions from the government. We believe that it is also a priority for the government to protect us from religions, as stated in the Constitution. Each and every time religions prove to be in contrast and in nonacceptance of the laws put in place by a voting majority, there should be a determination on whether any of these contrasting issues directly harms, disfigures or suppresses other Beings. There is a determining factor on whether a group, which shares a belief, has the right to make their belief surpass the laws. There are mainly two case scenarios of belief systems which are in contradiction with one another, and led us to the strong belief that depending on which group they belong to, they should be allowed to be above the laws or not. An example is the difference between the right of slaves not to be owned and the right of a person to own slaves. In the first case, the right of people not to be slaves should be granted because they are choosing what to do with themselves and themselves alone. In the second case, the choice directly affects other Beings, and denies the rights of those other Beings to choose for themselves.

Many religions today claim the religious right to make permanent decisions for their children or other sorts of abusive decisions towards other Beings, particularly women. We realize the importance of people having the right to their system of beliefs, however colorful these beliefs may be, and that right should be upheld as long as it does not take the rights away from other Beings.

Rules derived from a cultural upbringing are often similar to the rules derived from religious teachings; however, governments do not share the same compliance in the form of allowing the same special benefits. This means that when people base their choices on their cultural domestication they tend not to be granted the same acceptance from the western governments. Political correctness[40], on the other hand, shields cultural domestication from being addressed, and that makes it even more of a responsibility for Intentional Beings, who are protected by this benevolent shield, to act as responsible Beings and question the effects of the teachings that come from their cultural background. A Spiritual Seeker will question all that the establishment has indoctrinated into them, rather than accepting any of it without conscious examination. We are evolving creatures—what we believe to be right today is merely in accordance to the point of evolution we are at and the information currently available to us. Spiritual Evolution brings change, and our willingness to accept this change has to be constant.

---

40 See: *The Manual of Spiritual Living, Part 2: The Eve of Transformation....* Political Correctness

Sigmund Freud has done a thorough research regarding human behavior to try to understand how the human psyche works. This led him to learn customs and beliefs from different groups of people from all over the globe. In one of his books he creates a perspective based on two different and contrasting beliefs. One of the tribes that he came into contact with believed that as a form of love, respect, and in an attempt to create an ever-lasting bond with their loved ones in the moment of death, they ate them. This was considered a sacred act and for these people. In their view, the act of not consuming their dead was just as controversial as the act of cannibalism is for modern-day society.

The decision on wether or not to honor the belief of the tribe in consuming the deceased, as apposed to disposing of the corpses, is up to the majority of the people in a democratic system. When the majority has made their decision, it then overrules the religious beliefs of the minority. The majority of the people vote, in order to decide whether or not they consider it a right for a minority of people to pay their respects the way they see fit, or to consider some ways of paying the respects unacceptable, and therefore to make them illegal. At this point the religious minority must accept this decision and if they feel that this decision is wrong, attempt to change the minds of the majority of the people through peaceful, respectful, and considerate persuasion.

*A belief or political system that is not
evolving has no future.*

24

AWAKENING

❧

The amount of Awakening that one can experience is in direct proportion to the amount of awareness one is willing to bring into their life.

❧

Awakening is a process that takes place when we realize who we are without the conditioning from our domestications. The term, awakening, is commonly used in the New-Age community because of the resemblance to the act of awakening from a deep sleep and the realization that the dream we were experiencing is different from our waking reality. Similarly, we can realize that we are not the physical construct of our domestications, but the Spiritual, boundless soul living within this physical construct.

Awakening is the act of consciously waking up the dormant consciousness within. As we awaken, we become aware that what we know is not limited to what we have learned or experienced throughout this lifetime.

The main difference between remembering and awakening is in the fact that remembering does not mean to become completely awake. Evolving Spiritual Seekers begin remembering (regaining awareness that their consciousness pre-dates their life in a physical form) and the more they awaken, the more they remember.

༄

Awakening is when Spiritual Seekers accept the knowledge derived from remembering and remain in a state of awake-ness.

༄

25

INTUITON

The Manual of Spiritual Living extensively focuses on the tremendous capacity of Human Beings to gain knowledge through *feeling* it. Intuition is the act of perceiving knowledge without the aide of the rational mind. Intuition includes a wide variety of abilities that Human Beings can tap into. Males and females of the human race both have access to this wonderful capacity; however, intuition is considered to be a capacity that arises more from the right side of the brain. The right side of the brain is the more feminine part. The left side is the rational side and is considered to be the more masculine part.

All capacities that humans have access to can be cultivated by both genders, as both genders have access to these capacities. When it comes to the usage of the right and left side of the brain, the important thing to understand is that they are complementary. As gifted as an individual may be with one or the other, the results that they will be able to achieve without balancing the two will always be limited by the one ability between the two that they are less in touch with. As important as the rational seems to be, and how much we value and honor it and recommend all Human Beings to do so to, rational power is second to the greatest of all powers, which humans in this current physical evolution have access to. That is intuition.

"It is through science that we prove, but through intuition that we discover." — Henri Poincaré

Many truly gifted scientists like Albert Einstein and Leonardo Da Vinci have had amazing rational minds, which allowed them to make a multitude of their ideas into functioning projects or prototypes. Intuition, however, was the source of their ideas; without which, they would not have had anything to rationalize upon. Creativity, art, imagination, ideas, inventions, original thoughts— they are all the direct result of our intuitive capacity. Intuition is the spark; it makes no difference how much wood (knowledge) we are able to stack up, because without the spark (intuition), the fire will not light. Each and every single invention has been the consequence of an idea which was sparked by the creative self.

Sometimes too much knowledge can keep the creative spark from igniting. Humans have a tremendous capacity to memorize information. Every human that goes to school learns to memorize, and by the time they have graduated from University they have become very good at memorizing. In other words, they have absorbed the information, understood the mental process on how to apply it and consequently re-offer the services which the information they have acquired allows them to offer. This is functional in many ways, but can also be limiting in others ways as the brains are trained to remain confined to the process of thoughts that were learned. Any information that was acquired is restricted to reusing the same process of thought to process the new information when it becomes available. This limits the validity of the new information available to the judgement of others known to use the same processing and communicating techniques.

A fitting example of how there is an aspect of limiting the creativity of Humans Being induced by a restricting way of educating perpetrated by most schools and Universities is in the fact that many companies now purposely hire individuals to fill creative positions who have a background degree in something other than what they are being hired to do. This gives them an 'untainted' perspective, and companies have begun to value originality over repetition.

Our brains are wonderful tools but they tend to be domesticated like the muscles in the body. And just as the body will memorize a pattern of movement, the brain memorizes patterns of thought. In doing so, it will only excel in repeating those thoughts or movements which it has learned to repeat. Intuition is the act of being able to feel the messages of the body and the messages from the Collective Consciousness. In order to receive a wider spectrum of information, one must attempt to enable the brain to perform an unlimited range of thoughts. We have witnessed that in most cases humans who are subjected for long periods of time to prioritize the use of learned academic thought processes over the use of intuition lose their capacity to utilize this important gift. Similarly, most people who, for a long period of time, ignore the capacity to rationalize what they feel intuitively lose the capacity to make their intuitive understandings into useful objective resources.

The Scientific Method is considered the foundation of western medicine. It is a wonderful and quite reliable method which has the premise to find results as a consequence of demonstrable experimentation. Alternative medicine often has a different approach; the result is foreseen intuitively and finding the demonstrable scientific process which leads to that result is of secondary importance. The first method is relying on the premise that the result is null unless accompanied by a process which proves it to be scientifically true. The second method relies on the premise that if something seems to work, it does not really matter to be able to understand what makes it work and how to obtain a consistent result. (This is indeed a generalization, on our part, of how things are. We use this generalization intentionally, for the purpose of showing a clear image of the bigger picture.)

We feel that the success of both western and alternative medicine has been limited by the lack of recognition and balance of their intuitive and rational capacities. Many forms of alternative medicine are resulting directly from intuitive approaches. These alternative practitioners rely on their capacity to perceive energy flowing in the body and focus their attention in promoting techniques that allow this energy to keep flowing. The intuitive approach has the potential to speed up the process of human understanding ten fold. This potential, however, will be expressed only if objective reasoning can be added to the equation and if all of the limiting taboos set in place by the ego's of many groups of people, including the intuitive with their alternative medicine and the rational with their allopathic medicine, can be overcome.

In order to access intuition some people may initially benefit from asking themselves an internal question: How does this make me feel? Look at a bunch of organic tomatoes in a grocery store or at the farmer's market, and repeatedly ask yourself: How do these tomatoes make me feel? Look at the sky, take a deep breath and repeatedly ask yourself: How does this make me feel? Do the same thing with plants and other easy to spot beautiful, natural things. Establish a connection with those things that more intuitive beings before have approached and agreed upon the fact that they have a more vibrant energy and much alternative technology has corroborated this information. This process works like any other kind of exercise. In other words, feel what the kirlian[41] photographic images can show.

---

41 Also known as electrophotography. Kirlian photography can record the auric fields and energy of electromagnetic objects.

At first, like many new things, accessing intuition may seem frustrating, pointless, and without results. Yet, it is a huge force within us just waiting to explore and expand itself from within into all that is around. When not repressed by mental conditioning, fear, or other attempts of unacknowledgment, intuition will arise. It is not just a part of us, it is the most important part of who we are. It is the most pure form of Boundless Consciousness that we are, not that we have. It is the part within that does not question because it knows all that is known. Once the feeling of perceiving the energy of natural, beautiful things has become within one's realm of obvious understanding then one can extend it to other Beings, sounds, smells, feelings, words, actions, memories, emotions, relationships, intentions, decisions, projects, and so on.

Connect to all things using intuition— this is the most powerful action that we can do to evolve. In order to make it become relevant, be sure to combine it with impeccable objective reasoning. Learn the difference between something that feels good because it is good, rather than because it conveniently fills up a small void within us. Dedicate much integrity to distinguishing between true intuition and the intense desire to conveniently remain in ones comfort zone. Confront the validity of the information that makes us feel good with the intuitive perception of this information, in order to learn to discern the difference between the capacity to feel our intuitive self from the misguided experience of preserving the egotistical self.

Intuition is our link through which we give and take with the part that knows. It is the capacity of our higher self to express itself. Intuition can access the part that knows and use the information to guide us, but it is also the experimental part within that must decipher new information and judge the validity of this information through a process of feeling it. It is also our contribution to the expansion of the part that knows. Intuition expresses itself through creativity. Creativity is the art of creating. We are co-creators and our contribution is to add onto what has already been created. Each and every time we create an original thought (not a repeated concept) or a constructive variation of another thought we are adding this creation to the Collective Consciousness.

ENDNOTE

We will encourage the Spiritual Seekers to make the
search for truth a part of who they are and ask that
they bring impeccability to this search.
Impeccability begins from within as an inner
impeccability that is achieved through practice.

About the Authors

Gio and Heather are a living embodiment of Spiritual Living. He was born in the fashion capital of the world, Milan, Italy where he met Heather who was a fashion model. She was born in Calgary, Canada, and moved to Italy to be with Gio. It was there, in the land of romance, that they fell deeply in love. It was through this love that their Spiritual Path was born. Their union inspired them to explore new levels of consciousness which brought them to experience a heightened Spiritual Awakening. This eventually led them to leave behind their life of high fashion, clubs, fashion shows, and photo shoots to begin their Spiritual Adventure. After years of discovery and personal transformations, they felt the responsibility to share all that they have learned with others in order to contribute to the improvement of the world and the creatures living here. They now dedicate their life to their Spiritual Path, which includes sharing and learning with others.

This book has been created to make this world a better place for all beings.